SpringerBriefs in Economics

More information about this series at http://www.springer.com/series/8876

Zoltán J. Ács • László Szerb • Esteban Lafuente
Ainsley Lloyd

Global Entrepreneurship and Development Index 2018

Springer

Zoltán J. Ács
Center for Entrepreneurship and Public Policy
School of Public Policy
George Mason University
Arlington, VA, USA

László Szerb
Department of Quantitative Sciences
Faculty of Business and Economics
University of Pécs
Pécs, Hungary

Esteban Lafuente
Department of Management
Universitat Politècnica de Catalunya
(UPC Barcelona Tech) EPSEB
Barcelona, Spain

Ainsley Lloyd
The Global Entrepreneurship and
Development Institute
Washington, DC, USA

ISSN 2191-5504 ISSN 2191-5512 (electronic)
SpringerBriefs in Economics
ISBN 978-3-030-03278-4 ISBN 978-3-030-03279-1 (eBook)
https://doi.org/10.1007/978-3-030-03279-1

Library of Congress Control Number: 2018961563

This Springer imprint is published by the registered company Springer Nature Switzerland AG
The registered company address is: Gewerbestrasse 11, 6330 Cham, Switzerland

Foreword: A Compass for Strengthening Entrepreneurship Ecosystems

There is not a nation on earth that does not seek to nurture its doers, innovators, and makers of things. However, 2017 brings a new importance and sense of urgency to the development of one global entrepreneurship ecosystem.

At the Global Entrepreneurship Network (GEN), we have the privilege of guiding extensive global verticals and platforms around entrepreneurship research, policy approaches to start and scale new businesses, and grassroots entrepreneurial support programs. GEN also connects communities of mentors, investors, and founders who are working hard to keep pace with their rivals and new dynamic startup communities. Over the past 12 months, we have observed three important trends.

First, the world is now wide-awake to the notion of digital disruption. We are exiting an era of innovation defined by simple, on-demand consumer convenience apps and entering a chapter about the much more difficult process of disrupting highly regulated industries.

Thanks in part to programs like Global Entrepreneurship Week and Startup Weekend, the last 10 years have delivered a huge global army of enthusiastic nascent entrepreneurs organized in vibrant communities—but policymakers have been slower in responding. Early adaptors such as Airbnb and Uber disrupted long-standing traditional industries, while local, state, and federal policymakers around the world were caught off guard in understanding the public policy implications of such dramatic innovation.

This is just the tip of the iceberg of the digital disruption revolution unfolding.

Creating a new generation of globally competitive traditional industries will require a willingness of companies to either self-disrupt or deeply engage with the novices working on doing what they do better, faster, and cheaper. In addition, it will require a whole new approach from government—which brings us to our second trend in 2017.

The promise of jobs and economic growth and the optimism and hope that entrepreneurs bring to government efforts to create opportunity and prosperity for their citizens have generated an extraordinary increase in attention from all levels of government in empowering their entrepreneurial ecosystems.

At GEN Global, this explosion of public sector interest in high-growth entrepreneurship has fueled exciting new developments such as a 3-year agreement with the US government to form a policy staff secretariat to host a ministerial summit on entrepreneurial growth each March, the expansion of GEN's Startup Nations communities of startup savvy policy advisors, and the development of an international research community to fill the gaps in data and knowledge identified by decisionmakers looking for smarter policy instruments. In 2017, we expect to see the emergence of working groups that seek to anticipate and tackle likely policy dilemmas fueled by new disruptive technologies and incumbent displacements.

Similarly, entrepreneurs will increasingly focus on becoming more familiar with public policy as they enter highly regulated industries that simply do not operate effectively without clear collaboration between those setting the incentives and those disrupting the markets they were established to help thrive.

Finally, an anti-globalization sentiment is emerging as the most dominant case for accelerating our efforts at developing one global entrepreneurial ecosystem. I have traveled to more than 100 nations and spoken to entrepreneurs, investors, public policy leaders, and hundreds of private sector organizations enabling them. They are remarkable in their common language, vision, and values. They are almost all generous, optimistic, open, smart, and global.

But whether you see rising nationalism driving Brexit, Putin's Russia, America's flirtation with Trumpism, or other signals from countries tightening their borders and increasing their intolerance of free markets, the democratization of entrepreneurship has never been more important. Only through knowledge sharing and crowdsourcing can we really attack our common challenges as a planet.

One important force remains. It is still an interdependent global economy. Nations care about being competitive, and they will remain keen to engage with others and learn how to remain economically relevant and dynamic. The Global Entrepreneurship Index offers a means of comparing apples to apples and is an important element in guiding decisionmakers as they seek to build stronger entrepreneurial ecosystems that deliver the global prosperity we all seek.

Global Entrepreneurship Network Jonathan Ortmans
Washington, DC, USA

About the Global Entrepreneurship and Development Institute

The Global Entrepreneurship and Development Institute (GEDI) is the leading research organization advancing knowledge on the relationship between entrepreneurship, economic development, and prosperity. The Institute, headquartered in Washington D.C., was founded by leading entrepreneurship scholars from George Mason University, the University of Pécs, Imperial College London, and the London School of Economics. The Institute's flagship project is the Global Entrepreneurship Index (GEI), a breakthrough advance in measuring the quality and dynamics of entrepreneurship ecosystems at a national and regional level. The GEI methodology, on which the data in this report is based, has been validated by rigorous academic peer review and has been widely reported in the media, including in *The Economist*, *The Wall Street Journal*, *Financial Times*, and *Forbes*. The Institute's research has been funded by the European Union, the World Bank, and major corporations and banks around the world.

The Global Entrepreneurship and Development Institute
Arlington, VA, USA

Zoltán J. Ács

Contents

List of Figures

List of Tables

Chapter 1
The Entrepreneurial Ecosystem

Introduction

When the unemployment rate in the United States was 10% during the great recession, it was considered a catastrophe. However, the unemployment rate in most MENA countries is close to 30% and even higher in some other countries. This is a disaster for many parts of the world. It leads to desperation and violence as millions of youth struggle to survive. The world needs to create a billion jobs in the very near future to create global peace and prosperity. Entrepreneurship creates jobs and generates economic growth—the underpinning of a stable and civil society. But before we get into how this works, we need to discuss what kind of entrepreneurship we are talking about. Who is an entrepreneur? We are not talking about the basket weaver solo entrepreneur; we are not talking about rural microcredit. We are talking about Silicon Valley, Bill Gates, Sam Walton, FedEx, and Starbucks.

What Is Entrepreneurship?

An entrepreneur is a person with the vision to see an innovation and the ability to bring it to market. Most small business owners on main street in the United States or in the markets of most cities around the world are not entrepreneurs according to this definition. If you walk down the streets of Seventh Avenue in New York City, you will see street vendors selling the fare of every country in the world, nail shops, and small grocery stores. Few of these establishments are entrepreneurial by our definition because there is nothing new about them. Most of these people are traders or shop owners, performing a sort of small business management. Now these people

Z. J. Ács et al., *Global Entrepreneurship and Development Index 2018*, SpringerBriefs in Economics, https://doi.org/10.1007/978-3-030-03279-1_1

are important; don't get us wrong, they create jobs and income for their families. But we want to make a distinction here between the small business owner who replicates what others are doing and an entrepreneur who innovates.

Our definition of entrepreneurship is driven not by necessity entrepreneurship but by opportunity. Opportunity entrepreneurship is positively correlated with economic growth. Entrepreneurs envision scalable, high-growth businesses. They also possess the ability to make those visions a reality. They get things done. They go over, under, and around obstacles. This is borne out in the relationship observed between regulation and these two categories of entrepreneurs: regulation holds back replicative entrepreneurs but does not have the same impact on opportunity entrepreneurs. Entrepreneurs are the bridge between invention and commercialization. Invention without entrepreneurship stays in the university lab or the R&D facility. Entrepreneurs like Steve Jobs and Bill Gates commercialize other people's inventions. This vision of entrepreneurship actually delivers a product to customers.

While we have drawn a rather narrow definition of the entrepreneur, someone who innovates and gets things done, it is actually very broad. Entrepreneurs are everywhere, in every society, in rich and poor neighborhoods; they are Christians, Muslims, and Jews, male and female, gay and straight. They are people of color. Entrepreneurs can be high tech or low tech or even no tech. All over the world, entrepreneurs work in all sorts of conditions against great odds—in the slums of Kibera, Bombay, and Jakarta. They find ways to innovate and bring products to market. Just because entrepreneurs don't have access to finance, intellectual property protection, or a trained staff does not mean that entrepreneurs do not exist and cannot succeed. For example, Beleza Natural, which started with a single salon in 1993 in San Paulo, Brazil, currently operates 29 salons and a cosmetics research lab, produces a full line of hair-care products, and employs 1400 people. In 2012, the company's revenue was more than $30 million. Beleza Natural is interesting because it focused its activities on the demand of an overlooked group, in this case low-income women at the bottom of the pyramid. By offering "affordable luxuries" in the form of hair treatment and the salon experience, Beleza Natural was tapping into the so-called lipstick economy. However, as is the case for other successful female entrepreneurs, Beleza Natural aspired to provide greater benefits to its clients and employees. The company's business objectives extend to broader social and environmental benefits.[1]

A second aspect of our definition of entrepreneurship regards the level of technology. In the West, innovation is used synonymously with technology. The heroes in the West are Zuckerberg, Jobs, and other Silicon Valley stalwarts. Our definition is open to non-tech innovators like Oprah and Bowker. Starbucks serves a centuries-old drink, coffee, but it introduced a coffee shop experience that is now in every corner of the world. When you go into Starbucks and there is a long line, it disappears in just a few minutes. That is process innovation and very much an example of a non-tech entrepreneur. McDonalds did the same for the hamburger. Enterprise

[1]Acs Z., and P. Correa. The World Bank and GEDI, Identifying the Obstacles to High-Impact Entrepreneurship in Latin America and the Caribbean, (2014).

Rent-A-Car did it for car rentals and today employs thousands of people worldwide. Uber did it for taxicabs. They did not invent taxis. They have been around forever. They invented a new process. What low-tech entrepreneurship does is increase efficiency: how quickly you can serve a cup of coffee.

Entrepreneurial Ecosystem Elements

Ever since the time of Schumpeter, the concepts of entrepreneurship and innovation have been intertwined with economic development. The Global Entrepreneurship Development Index is an important tool to help countries accurately assess and evaluate their ecosystem to create more jobs. The *entrepreneurial ecosystem* is a new way to contextualize the increasingly complex and interdependent social systems being created.[2] While the academic literature kept agency, institutions, and systems in separate silos, the real communities that practitioners worked in had no such silos and the different building blocks all built upon each other in a single, unified structure. Business books such as Brad Feld's *Start-up communities: Building an Entrepreneurial Ecosystem in Your City,* Daniel Isenberg's *Harvard Business Review* article *What an entrepreneurship ecosystem actually is*, and Steven Koltai, *Peace through Entrepreneurship: Investing in a Start-up Culture for Security and Development*, started to suggest that reality was nuanced.

In order to better understand entrepreneurial ecosystems, let's start with a few definitions. A system is an organized set of interacting and interdependent subsystems that function together as a whole to achieve a purpose. In general, an ecosystem is a purposeful collaborating network of dynamic interacting systems and subsystems that have an ever-changing set of dependencies within a given context. First, an ecosystem, as opposed to a system, has both living and nonliving components. Otherwise it's a system like national systems of innovation. In addition, there are outcomes of the ecosystem that the literature calls ecosystem services, and there is ecosystem management. The point of this line of research is that it is not just the abundance or endowment of particular key factors of production or resources that shapes economic performance; it is also the manner in which that economic activity is configured, or organized, within geographic space.

The most carefully worked out approach to entrepreneurial ecosystems is associated with Acs, Szerb, and Autio (2014a). This line of research recognizes that it is not just the abundance or endowment of particular key factors of production or resources that shapes economic performance; it is also the manner in which that economic activity is configured, or organized, within geographic space and the role of entrepreneurship in bringing it to life. While the entrepreneurial ecosystem literature does not challenge the efficacy of these other dimensions of spatial organization and structure, such as clusters, specialization, diversity, market power, or localized

[2] Acs, Autio, and Szerb, (2014b), Autio, Kenney, Mustar, Siegel, and Wright, (2014).

competition, it suggests that entrepreneurship is also a key dimension enhancing economic performance.

Entrepreneurial ecosystems are composed of subsystems (pillars) that are aggregated into systems (sub-indices) that can be optimized for system performance at the ecosystem level. There is a growing recognition in the entrepreneurship literature that entrepreneurship theory focused only on the entrepreneur may be too narrow. The concept of systems of entrepreneurship is based on three important premises that provide an appropriate platform for analyzing entrepreneurial ecosystems. First, entrepreneurship is fundamentally an action undertaken and driven by agents on the basis of incentives. Second, the individual action is affected by an institutional framework conditions. Third, entrepreneurship ecosystems are complex, multifaceted structures in which many elements interact to produce systems performance; thus, the index method needs to allow the constituent elements to interact. However, because the elements are different in each case, there is no one-size-fits-all solution. Each one is bespoke.

The Global Entrepreneurship Ecosystem

We define entrepreneurial ecosystems at the socioeconomic level having properties of self-organization, scalability, and sustainability as "…dynamic institutionally embedded interaction between entrepreneurial attitudes, abilities and aspirations, by individuals, which drives the allocation of resources through the creation and operation of new ventures."[3] Entrepreneurial Ecosystems are complex socioeconomic structures that are brought to life by individual-level action. Much of the knowledge relevant for entrepreneurial action is embedded in ecosystem structures and requires individual-level action to extract it.[4]

The structure of the entrepreneurial ecosystem is illustrated in Fig. 1.1. Nascent and new entrepreneurs are at the heart of the system. Nascent entrepreneurs are individuals in the process of launching a new venture. These entrepreneurs represent a subset of the adult population in a given country. The attitudes that prevail within the wider population influence who chooses to become an entrepreneur. The nascent and new entrepreneurs are characterized by varying degrees of ability and entrepreneurial aspirations.

It is the entrepreneurs who drive the trial-and-error dynamic. This means entrepreneurs start businesses to pursue opportunities that they themselves perceive. However, entrepreneurs can't tell in advance if opportunities are real or not.

[3] Acs, Szerb and Autio, National Systems of Entrepreneurship: Measurement and Policy, Research Policy, (2014b:479).

[4] Stakeholder engagement is central for multi-polar policy-making and implementation. Deep stakeholder engagement can tap knowledge within the ecosystem and uncover hidden interactions and cause-effect chains.

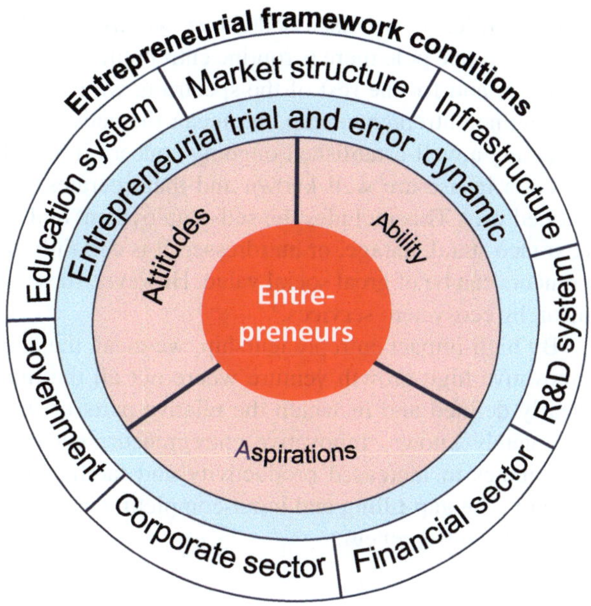

Fig. 1.1 The Entrepreneurial Ecosystem Configuration

The only way to validate an opportunity is to pursue it. The outcome is a trial-and-error process.

The entrepreneurial framework conditions matter because they regulate first who chooses to become an entrepreneur and, second, to what extent the resulting new ventures are able to fulfill their growth potential. The first aspect—entrepreneurial choice—is regulated mostly by soft framework conditions, such as social norms and cultural preferences. The degree to which new ventures are able to fulfill their potential is regulated by a range of entrepreneurial framework conditions, such as government, research and development, education, infrastructure, financial sector, and the corporate sector.

A healthy entrepreneurial ecosystem will drive resource allocation toward productive uses. It will also drive total factor productivity through process innovation (Starbucks). The greater total factor productivity, the greater the economy's capacity to create jobs and wealth.

Agents

The first component of entrepreneurial ecosystems is agency. The entrepreneur drives the system. The entrepreneur is someone who makes judgment-based decisions about the coordination of scarce resources. The term "someone" is defined as the individual, and the term "judgment-based decisions" is a decision for which no obviously correct procedure exists. Judgment is not the routine application of a standard rule. As we discussed above, we distinguish two types of entrepreneurial activity: at one pole there is routine entrepreneurship, which is really a type of management, and for the rest of the spectrum, we have high-growth entrepreneurship. By routine entrepreneurship, we mean the activities involved in coordinating and executing a well-established ongoing concern in which the parts of the production function in use are well known and that operates in well-established and clearly defined way. This includes the self-employment and small business owner. It is the next taco stand, garage, or hairdresser. It is certainly the case that replicative entrepreneurs can be of great social value. However, these types of firms are not what we mean by ecosystem services.[5]

By high-impact entrepreneurship, we mean the activities necessary to create an innovative high-growth venture where not all the markets are well established or clearly defined and in which the relative parts of the production function are not completely known. Innovative entrepreneurs ensure that utilization of invention contributes to increased productivity and facilitates and contributes to economic growth. The gap-filling and input-completing capacities are the unique characteristics of the entrepreneur.

Institutions

The second fundamental component of entrepreneurial ecosystems is institutions—the rules of the game. Of particular importance to entrepreneurship are the economic institutions in society such as the structure of property rights and the presence of effective market frameworks. Economic institutions are important because they influence the structure of economic incentives. Without property rights, individuals will not have the incentive to invest in physical or human capital or adopt more efficient technologies. Economic institutions are also important because they help to allocate resources to their most efficient uses; they determine who gets profits, revenues, and residual rights of control. When markets were highly restricted and institutions sent the wrong signals, there is little substitution between labor and capital, and technological change is minimal.

Institutions create incentives, and the entrepreneurial talent is allocated to activities with the highest private return, which need not have the highest social returns. Universal welfare-enhancing outcomes do not automatically follow from entrepreneurial activity; indeed such activities can generate questionable or undesirable effects. Entrepreneurial talent can be allocated among a range of choices with varying effects from wealth creation to destruction of economic welfare. If the same actor can become engaged in such alternative activities, then the mechanism through

[5]While there is a small literature on entrepreneurship and economic growth our view is that high-impact firms cause economic growth because they shift the production function and replicative entrepreneurship is caused by economic growth and creates employment by replicating the existing production function.

which talent is allocated has important implications for economic outcomes, and the quality of this mechanism is the key criterion in evaluating a given set of institutions with respect to growth.

We follow many others, for example, Hayek, in proposing that the answer rests upon the institutional system and the incentives that it creates for agents; yet we differ in simultaneously stressing the role of entrepreneurs. In the United States, institutions of private property and contract enforcement give entrepreneurs the incentive to invest in physical and human capital, to combine inputs in ways to create new production functions, and to complete markets. It is entrepreneurs operating in supportive institutional environments that provide the transmission mechanism from knowledge to economic growth by raising productivity.

The System

The third component of entrepreneurial ecosystems is the systems. When we look at systems, for example, systems of innovation or clusters, we have a theory of how the system functions as it produces outputs. Porter's Diamond comes to mind. When we move to an ecosystem, we also need to have a theory of how the ecosystem functions. How does an entrepreneurial ecosystem function? It is not enough to have a laundry list of the institutions that might be important: markets, human capital, supports culture, finance, and policy. While all of these may be important, how they work as an ecosystem is missing in much of this literature.

Building on the systems of innovation literature and the Global Entrepreneurship Monitor methodology, we develop an entrepreneurial ecosystem that integrates both institutions and agency and introduce an ecosystem of coherent patterns in a simple, intuitive, and powerful way. The key ideas are the relationships; the complementary, across the systems and subsystems; and the importance of bottleneck factors. The concept of complementary in its simplest way is the interaction of two variables. Two-choice variables are complements, when doing more of one of them increases the returns to doing more of the other. Figure 1.2 shows the pillars of the entrepreneurial ecosystem for factor-driven economies on three continents and compares them to one another. Risk capital is always hard but not impossible even in factor-driven economies.

Ecosystem Services

While many think of the output of ecosystems as more startups, like GEM, this is wrong and misleading. The dual service created by entrepreneurial ecosystems is (1) resource allocation toward productive uses and (2) the innovative, high-growth ventures that drive this process. The entrepreneurship literature frequently talks about opportunity recognition and the need to assemble resources. However, from a

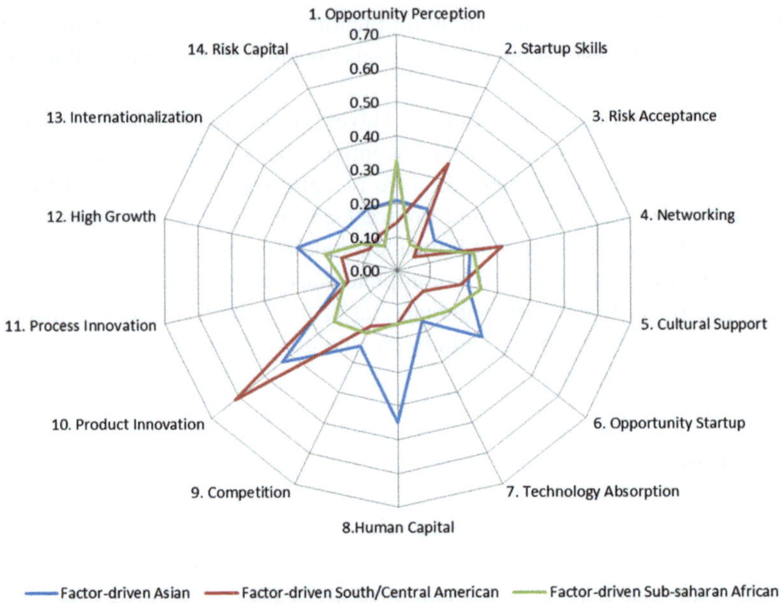

Fig. 1.2 Factor-driven economies at the pillar level

performance perspective, the key issue is about resource allocation from existing activities to new ones. The allocation of resources to productive uses will result in high-growth, high-value new firms. The nutrient in the ecosystem is resources—venture capital! Without nutrients, the ecosystem will die. For example, the launch of Uber and Airbnb early this decade and the earlier success of Google, Amazon, Facebook, Twitter, Skype, WhatsApp, and Craigslist created a new breed of company. The billion-dollar tech startup was once the stuff of myth, but now they seem to be everywhere, backed by a bull market, readily available venture capital, and a new generation of disruptive technology.[6]

Ecosystem Management

In the ecological literatures, the practice of managing and enhancing ecosystem benefits is referred to as ecosystem management. Because ecosystem services is created through a myriad of localized interactions between stakeholders, it is not

[6]This trend is reflected in the continuing decline in the cost of computing, the rise of open-source software, the move to the 'cloud' and the emergence of huge datacenters where companies such as Amazon, Google, and Facebook are designing their own approaches.

easy to trace gaps in system performance back to specific, well-defined market and structural failures that could be addressed in a top-down mode.[7]

Strengthening the entrepreneurial ecosystem can be done by public-private partnerships, banks, universities, foundations, governments, and aid agencies. The Global Entrepreneurial Ecosystem Roadmap (GEER) focuses on the first aspect of this project, that is, (1) identifying the holes in the global entrepreneurship ecosystem, (2) laying out a roadmap for how to fill in the holes, and (3) measuring our progress. The goal of a well-functioning ecosystem is to improve the chances of success for entrepreneurs all over the world and ultimately reduce unemployment and bring peace to the world.

References

Acs, Z. J., Szerb, L., & Autio, E. (2014a). *The Global Entrepreneurship Index 2014*. Seattle: CreateSpace.

Acs, Z., Autio, E., & Szerb, L. (2014b). National Systems of entrepreurship: Measuremenat issue and policy implications. *Research Policy, 43*, 476–494.

Autio, E., & Levie, J. (2015). *Management of entrepreneurial ecosystems*. Mimeo: Imperial college Business School.

Autio, E., Kenney, M., Mustar, P., Siegel, D., & Wright, M. (2014). Entrepreneurial innovation: The importance of context. *Research Policy, 43*(7), 1097–1108.

[7] Autio and Levie (2015).

Chapter 2
The Entrepreneurial Ecosystem and Global Prosperity

Introduction

While a focus on the entrepreneurial ecosystem may seem a novel approach to development, it is consistent with and even complementary to older, more traditional development strategies. As developing economies move from centralized economies to market economies, enterprise and entrepreneurship become important. "The emerging world, long a source of cheap labor, now rivals developed countries for business innovation. Developing countries are becoming hotbeds of business innovation in much the same way as Japan did from the 1950s onwards."[1]

Entrepreneurship is considered an important mechanism that promotes economic development through employment, innovation, and welfare, but it does not appear like manna from heaven as a country moves through the stages of development. Rather, it plays a role in all development stages and is a process that continues over many years. Economists have come to recognize the "input-competing" and "gap-filling" capacities of entrepreneurial activity in development.[2] In other words, someone has to create the technology for new products and create the markets where people will buy them.

Two points are important when thinking about entrepreneurship and development. *First, contrary to popular belief, the most entrepreneurial countries in the world are not those that have the most entrepreneurs.* This notion is in fact misleading. In fact, the highest self-employment rates are in low-income countries such as Zambia and Nigeria. This is because low-income economies lack the human capital and infrastructure needed to create high-quality jobs. The result is that many people sell soft drinks and fruit on street corners, but there are few innovative, high-growth startups. Nor do these street vendors represent business ownership as defined in many developed countries.

---

[1] Woolridge (2009).

[2] Leibenstein (1968).

Z. J. Ács et al., *Global Entrepreneurship and Development Index 2018*,
SpringerBriefs in Economics, https://doi.org/10.1007/978-3-030-03279-1_2

In entrepreneurship, quality matters more than quantity. To be entrepreneurial, a country needs to have the best entrepreneurs, not necessarily the most. What the "best and the brightest" do is important, and to support their efforts, a country needs a well-functioning entrepreneurial ecosystem (watch the video).[3] The path to development is to create efficient organizations able to harness technology to increase output and improve the lives of millions.

Second, entrepreneurship comes in productive, unproductive, and destructive forms. While productive entrepreneurship makes both entrepreneurs and society better off, unproductive and destructive entrepreneurship makes entrepreneurs better off but leave society in worse condition. The GEI strives to measure only productive entrepreneurship that both creates wealth and is scalable.

Entrepreneurial ecosystems support innovative, productive, and rapidly growing new ventures. They consist of multiple interactive elements, all of which need to be in sync in order for innovative and high-growth firms to prosper. Such firms also need skilled employees. They need access to technology. They need a well-functioning infrastructure. They need specialized advice and support. They need access to finance. They need business premises. They need a supportive regulatory framework.

The Global State of Entrepreneurship

The GEI measures both the quality of entrepreneurship in a country and the extent and depth of the supporting entrepreneurial ecosystem. The map below presents a snapshot of the global entrepreneurial ecosystem (Fig. 2.1).

The top ten countries for 2018 show a pattern similar to last year's—high-income, mostly European nations. The top countries are the United States, Switzerland, Canada, Sweden, Denmark, Iceland, Australia, United Kingdom,

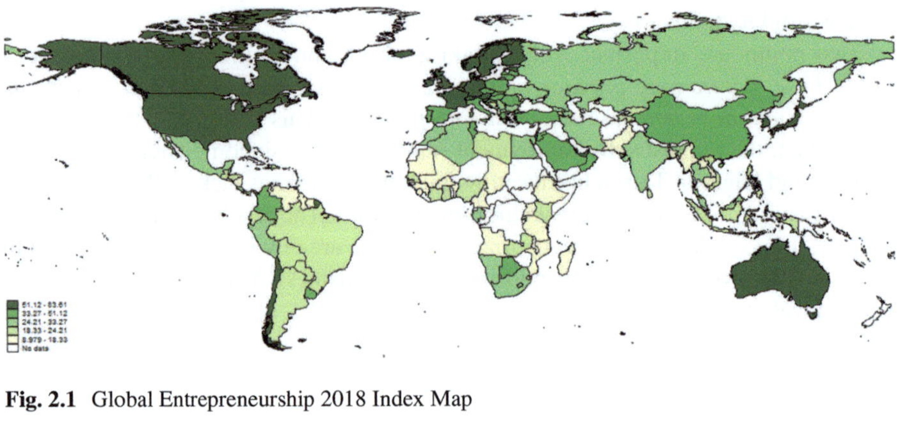

Fig. 2.1 Global Entrepreneurship 2018 Index Map

[3] https://www.youtube.com/watch?v=hjNc_BScn-s.

Ireland, and the Netherlands. The major surprise this year is the movement of Switzerland from eighth place to second; the United States remains first for the third year in a row. Because the scores in the highest range are so close, small changes in score from 1 year to the next can produce a relatively large shift in ranks among the top ten. For this reason, we present confidence intervals for the top ten.

Top Ten Countries (Table 2.1 and Fig. 2.2)

The results show that the No. 1 rank could have gone to any of the top eight nations with the exception of the United Kingdom and the Netherlands. We see that Switzerland has a confidence interval almost similar to the United States.

Regional Performance

For many countries, a regional benchmark is more relevant for identifying best practices for fostering entrepreneurship. This year we have several important changes in Europe, sub-Saharan Africa, and the MENA countries. Below we present the top performer in each region along with individual and institutional score summaries (Table 2.2).

The United States leads the world in entrepreneurship and is first in the North American region, just ahead of peer Canada. Australia ranks first in the Asia-Pacific region, ahead of economic powerhouses China, Singapore, Hong Kong, and Japan.

Table 2.1 Top ten countries in the GEI

Country	GEI 2018 lower limit	GEI 2018 upper limit	GEI 2018	Rank 2018	GEI Rank 2017	Rank 2017
United States	77.5	89.7	83.6	1	1	United States
Switzerland	72.5	88.4	80.4	2	2	Switzerland
Canada	73.9	84.6	79.2	3	3	Canada
United Kingdom	73.6	81.9	77.8	4	8	Sweden
Australia	69.0	82.0	75.5	5	7	Denmark
Denmark	64.8	83.8	74.3	6	5	Iceland
Iceland	63.6	84.7	74.2	7	6	Australia
Ireland	66.8	80.6	73.7	8	9	United Kingdom
Sweden	67.1	79.1	73.1	9	4	Ireland
France	59.9	77.1	68.5	10	13	Netherlands

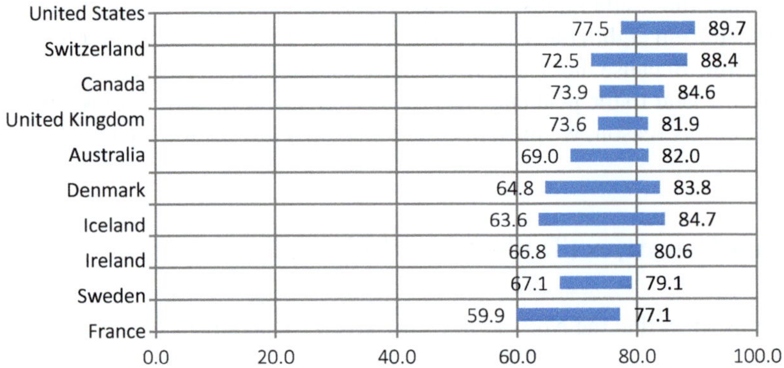

Fig. 2.2 Confidence intervals for top ten scores

Table 2.2 Top scores by region

World rank	Country	Region	GDP per capita PPP	Individual variables	Institutional variables	GEI
1	United States	North America	$52.676	93.0	78.5	83.6
2	Switzerland	Europe	$54.933	93.8	71.5	80.4
5	Australia	Asia-Pacific	$42.149	82.2	74.3	75.5
16	Israel	Middle East/North Africa	$31.092	80.9	72.7	65.4
19	Chile	South and Central America/Caribbean	$21.302	68.9	75.9	58.5
52	Botswana	Sub-Saharan Africa	$15.286	47.7	66.0	34.9

Switzerland, which ranked fourth in the European region and eighth overall last year, now comes in first in Europe. Chile ranks first in South and Central America and the Caribbean (16th overall), 19 places ahead of the next highest scorer in the region—Puerto Rico, at 35th. Israel is 17th overall and tops the MENA region, just ahead of UAE at 21st. In sub-Saharan Africa, Botswana is the leader at 52nd, ranking ahead of nine European nations.

Biggest Gains (Table 2.3)

Table 2.3 Biggest gains in GEI score

Country	Score 2018	Score 2017	Difference in score	Difference in rank
United Kingdom	77.8	71.2	6.5	4
Israel	65.4	59.4	6.0	1
Bulgaria	27.8	22.7	5.1	13
China	41.1	36.1	5.0	5
Iran	26.8	22.1	4.7	13
Italy	41.4	37.1	4.3	4
Poland	50.4	46.5	3.9	1
Canada	79.2	75.5	3.7	0
Ireland	73.7	70.2	3.5	1
Korea	54.2	50.7	3.5	3

Legend: includes only those countries that have participated in the GEM survey and do not have estimated individual data

Biggest Declines (Table 2.4)

Table 2.4 Biggest declines in GEI score (only with decreasing GEI scores)

Country	Score 2018	Score 2017	Difference in score	Difference in rank
Latvia	40.5	43.0	−2.5	−6
Sweden	73.1	75.2	−2.1	−5
Taiwan	59.5	61.0	−1.5	−2
Malaysia	32.7	33.4	−0.7	−4
Ecuador	20.5	20.9	−0.4	−5
Chile	58.5	58.9	−0.4	−1
Kazakhstan	29.7	30.0	−0.3	−2
Indonesia	21.0	21.1	−0.1	−4

Legend: includes only those countries that have participated in the GEM survey and do not have estimated individual data

Country-Level Productivity and the Entrepreneurial Ecosystem

Perhaps the first point that should be made in this subchapter is that economic growth does not equal to productivity. Economic growth basically refers to the capacity of countries to produce more goods and services, irrespective of how higher production is achieved. The positive variations in GDP or employment over time are the usual suspects among those interested in studying economic growth figures, mostly because they represent the desired objective of most policymakers, as a measure of economic prosperity.

Productivity is a more complex concept. At the country level, total factor productivity (TFP) deals with two highly interconnected economic aspects. First, TFP has to do with the capacity of countries to allocate and exploit available resources efficiently (*P* = productivity effect). The notion that markets are good at directing resources is a good catch-all explanation concept; but for many businesses, it is hard to find all that is required to perform in the market and to keep the pace of industrial and digital revolutions that not only equip businesses with new—often more technologically advanced—resources but also change the ways to exploit them.

The second component of TFP deal with the capacity of organizations to channel innovations to the economy (*I* = innovation effect) that, consequently, translate into higher levels of output per input unit (in the case of countries, GDP per worker). Maybe we all are too used to link innovation to technological inventions that are successfully commercialized. However, our definition of innovation is not restricted to engineering (such as the driverless car) or to medical advances (such as nerve stimulation or noninvasive procedures) and is open to other, equally valuable, types of non-technological innovations related to product and processes.

Let's start with the productivity effect (*P*). The efficient allocation of resources available in the economy is an important part of the productivity function. The productivity effect is linked to how well new and existing businesses use different resources, including labor, capital, equipment, knowledge, and technology-based inputs. The capacity of Amazon to amalgamate technologies brought from other industries (e.g., ICTs, drones) to increase the productivity of its operations (delivery: AmazonFresh or Amazon Prime Air) is a good example.[4]

From the perspective of the entrepreneurship ecosystem, better institutions backing entrepreneurial activities and an efficient interaction between individual actions and the institutional setting governing entrepreneurial decisions are key ingredients necessary to facilitate the creation of businesses with a greater capacity to generate jobs and help incumbent businesses to take advantage of better market conditions. For example, in many European countries, entrepreneurs have strong incentives to invest in physical and human capital and to promote the exploitation of resources in an effort to improve the functioning of their businesses. In this case, the supportive institutional environment creates the conditions to promote operational improvements. In other words, entrepreneurial ventures have incentives to "do things better," that is, to improve their productivity. To sum up, a healthy entrepreneurial ecosystem contributes to national productivity by enhancing market efficiency levels and by promoting the efficient exploitation of resources through new and incumbent businesses.[5]

---

[4] The Wall Street Journal (2014). 'Amazon Reports Loss Despite Strong Sales Growth'. Available at: http://online.wsj.com/articles/amazon-reports-another-loss-despite-strong-sales-growth-1406233529.

[5] Acs, Z.J., Autio, E., Szerb, L. (2014). National systems of entrepreneurship: Measurement issues and policy implications. Research Policy, 43(3), 476–494.

The second effect—innovation (*I*)—is strictly linked to the Schumpeterian approach to entrepreneurship (creative destruction).[6] For Schumpeter, entrepreneurs play a decisive role in the economy by creating and implementing radical innovations that are conducive to economic progress. In this tradition entrepreneurship is critical to spark economic development by promoting innovations, in our terminology "create new things or find new ways to do things." Progress translates in the expansion of the countries' production possibilities that materialize in a shift of the global frontier.

But, at this point is worth questioning how can radical innovations foster such progress. Moreover, how does the entrepreneurial ecosystem contribute to this progress? It seems logical to argue that inventions are worthless if they do not turn into commercialized innovations and that the economic impact of such innovations will turn sterile if the market and individuals cannot fully incorporate these innovations in their day-to-day routines.

For Schumpeter, entrepreneurs nurture the economy with innovations and the entrepreneurial ecosystem is critical for the development of this economic function: "create new things or find new ways to do things." If countries enjoy a healthy entrepreneurial ecosystem, the efforts of innovative entrepreneurs will materialize in new value-adding combinations of resources that will expand the countries' productive capacity and the global production frontier.

We found a significant, relatively strong positive correlation between entrepreneurship and total factor productivity (0.35). We also noted that entrepreneurship correlates weakly positively with the productivity effect (0.09). The strongest positive correlation was found between entrepreneurship and the innovation effect (0.39). This result is not surprising if we think a little harder. Just like we cannot imagine progress in the nineteenth century without the creation and development of steam engines, it is hard to imagine entrepreneurship in the twenty-first century without the power of technology-driven inventions. With the new millennium, industries and markets from all around the globe are witnessing drastic transformations that are the result of a digital revolution in which entrepreneurs are taking an active role by creating new businesses that are responsible of this revolution. The result is a good sign that reinforces our argument that the creation of "new things or new ways to do things" definitely constitutes the vital force driving economic development.

We also examined the connection between the GEI score and the computed total factor productivity values. The correlation between TFP and GEI is 0.35 and the sign is positive: the quality of the entrepreneurial ecosystem (GEI scores) and TFP moves in the same direction. Countries with a low-quality entrepreneurial ecosystem tend to show negative TFP values below unity. On contrary, all developed economies with supportive entrepreneurial ecosystems improve their total factor productivity, either by productivity or innovation effects.

---

[6] Schumpeter, J.A. (1934). The Theory of Economic Development: An Inquiry into Profits, Capital, Credit, Interest, and the Business Cycle. Cambridge, MA: Harvard University Press.

As noted earlier, there is a positive association between entrepreneurship and the productivity effect (correlation = 0.09); however, this relationship is less pronounced than that found for the TFP. This result may well be partly explained by the differentiating impact of entrepreneurship over the productivity effect across economies. We observe that the correlation between entrepreneurship and the productivity effect scores the highest among factor-driven countries (0.47). We also note that in many underdeveloped and developing territories with low- and mid-level entrepreneurial ecosystem, the productivity effect is positive, while the result of the productivity effect for some developed economies is negative. Thus, our results suggest that, in developing economies, the entrepreneurial ecosystem plays a much more decisive role on TFP via productivity improvements, that is, helping new and established businesses in developing economies to better exploit their limited resources, that is, "to do things better."

The picture is quite different when we look at the results for the innovation effect. The correlation between entrepreneurship and the innovation effect progressively increases as we move from factor-driven (correlation = −0.41) to innovation-driven economies (correlation = 0.33). Similarly, the impact of the innovation effect is much more potent in innovation-driven economies (1.55%) than in efficiency-driven (1.17%) and in factor-driven economies (−0.59%). In contrast to the stronger effect of the entrepreneurial ecosystem over productivity in developing countries, we found that the positive influence of a healthy entrepreneurial ecosystem over the innovative capacity of new and established businesses is much more powerful in developed economies. With the exception of Turkey, the innovation effect linked to the efficient commercialization of innovations and new technologies is positive in all economies with high-quality entrepreneurial ecosystems (GEI > 50).

Based on the relationships reported above, the improvement of the entrepreneurial ecosystem (GEI scores) may well yield to improvements in total factor productivity via the enhanced capacity of businesses to use their available resources (productivity effect) and to exploit the market potential of new technologies and innovations. As a result, if every of the 64 analyzed countries raised its GEI score by 10%, the global total factor productivity will increase 0.22 TFP points, which represents an estimated improvement of 15.80%.[7]

[7] We agree that correlation and basic regression coefficients are not enough to determine causation, which is why we say that a 10% global increase in GEI could improve global productivity 0.22 points. But, it should be kept in mind that the said change in the GEI, and the changes to institutions that it represents, could add this amount to global productivity, since the institutions that support entrepreneurship also support a variety of other economic and non-economic activities.

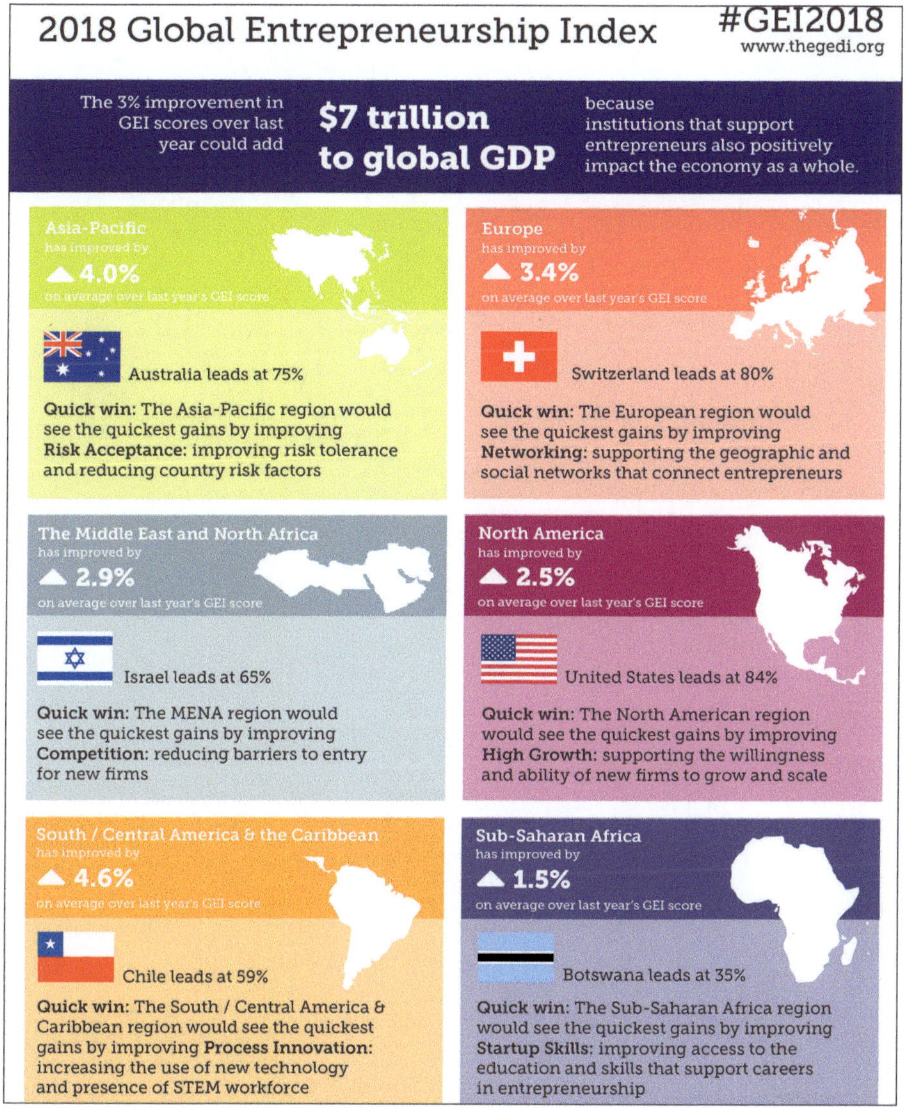

References

Leibenstein, H. (1968). Entrepreneurship and development. *American Economic Review, 38*(2), 72–83.

Woolridge, A. (2009, March 14). Global heroes: A special report on entrepreneurship. *The Economist*, 1–19.

Chapter 3
The Global Entrepreneurship and Development Index

The Fourteen Pillars of the Global Entrepreneurial and Development Index

The pillars of entrepreneurship in the ecosystem are many and complex. While a widely accepted definition of entrepreneurship is lacking, there is general agreement that the concept has numerous dimensions.[1] We take this into account in creating the entrepreneurship index. Some businesses have a larger impact on markets, create more new jobs, and grow faster and become larger than others. We also take into account the fact that entrepreneurship plays a different role at different stages of development.[2] Considering all of these possibilities and limitations, we define entrepreneurship as "the dynamic, institutionally embedded interaction between entrepreneurial attitudes, entrepreneurial abilities, and entrepreneurial aspirations by individuals, which drives the allocation of resources through the creation and operation of new ventures."

The GEI is composed of three building blocks or sub-indices—what we call the 3As: entrepreneurial attitudes, entrepreneurial abilities, and entrepreneurial aspirations. Entrepreneurial attitudes are about how a country thinks about entrepreneurship. In fact, what does your mother think about it? The second sub-index is about abilities. Can you do it? Do you have the skills? The third sub-index is about aspirations. Do you want to build a billion-dollar company? These three sub-indices stand on 14 pillars, each of which contains an individual and an institutional variable that corresponds to the micro- and the macro-level aspects of entrepreneurship. Unlike other indices that incorporate only institutional *or* individual variables, the pillars of the GEI include both. These pillars are an attempt to capture the open-ended nature

[1] Gartner (1990), Davidsson (2004), Wennekers and Thurik (1999), Godin, Clemens, and Veldhuis (2008), Zahra, et al. (2014), Gupta and Gupta (2015) all identify several dimensions of entrepreneurship.

[2] Baumol (1990), Vivarelli (2013), Thurik et al. (2013).

Z. J. Ács et al., *Global Entrepreneurship and Development Index 2018*,
SpringerBriefs in Economics, https://doi.org/10.1007/978-3-030-03279-1_3

of entrepreneurship; analyzing them can provide an in-depth view of the strengths and weaknesses of those listed in the index. We now describe the 14 pillars of entrepreneurship.

Entrepreneurial Attitudes Pillars

Pillar 1 *Opportunity Perception*. This pillar captures the potential "opportunity perception" of a population by considering the state of property rights and the regulatory burden that could limit the real exploitation of the recognized entrepreneurial opportunity. Within this pillar is the individual variable, Opportunity Recognition, which measures the percentage of the population that can identify good opportunities to start a business in the area where they live. However, the value of these opportunities also depends on the size of the market. The institutional variable Freedom and Property consists of two smaller variables: economic freedom (Economic Freedom) and property rights (Property Rights). Business Freedom—one sub-index of the Index of Economic Freedom variable—is appropriate for capturing the overall burden of regulation, as well as the government's regulatory efficiency in influencing startups and operating businesses. "The property rights element is an assessment of the ability of individuals to accumulate private property, secured by clear laws that are fully enforced by the state," or in other words, enforced property rights guarantee that individuals have the right to harvest the fruits of successful opportunity exploitation and no one is confiscating or stealing their property or business.[3] Both institutional components are vital for individuals to become entrepreneurs and not employees of another business or the state.[4]

Pillar 2 *Startup Skills*. Launching a successful venture requires the potential entrepreneur to have the necessary startup skills. Skill Perception measures the percentage of the population who believe they have adequate startup skills. Most people in developing countries think they have the skills needed to start a business, but their skills were usually acquired through workplace trial and error in relatively simple business activities. In developed countries, business formation, operation, management, etc. require skills that are acquired through formal education and training. Hence, education, especially postsecondary education, plays a vital role in teaching and developing entrepreneurial skills. Today there are 150 million students enrolled in some kind of education beyond high school, a 53 percent increase in less than a decade. People all over the world see education as a pathway out of poverty.[5]

Pillar 3 *Risk Acceptance*. Of the personal entrepreneurial traits, fear of failure is one of the most important obstacles to a startup. Aversion to high-risk enterprises can retard nascent entrepreneurship. Risk Perception is defined as the percentage of

[3] Bjørnskov and Foss (2010), Goel et al. (2015).

[4] Bhola, Verheul, Thurik, and Grilo (2006), Tumasjan and Braun (2012), Autio et al. (2014).

[5] Papagiannidis and Li (2005), Dutta, Li, and Merenda (2011), Ibrahim and Mas'ud (2016).

the population who do not believe that fear of failure would prevent them from starting a business. Country Risk reflects to transfer and convertibility risk of a country and believed to closely correlate to business.[6]

Pillar 4 *Networking.* Networking combines an entrepreneur's personal knowledge with their ability to connect to others in a country and the whole world. This combination serves as a proxy for networking, which is also an important ingredient of successful venture creation and entrepreneurship. Entrepreneurs who have better networks are more successful, can identify more viable opportunities, and can access more and better resources. We define the basic networking potential of a possible entrepreneur by the percentage of the population who personally know an entrepreneur who started a business within two years (Know Entrepreneurs). The connectivity variable has two components: One that measures the urbanization (Urbanization) of the country and the other measuring the quality of the transport infrastructure (Infrastructure).[7]

Pillar 5 *Cultural Support.* This pillar is a combined measure of how a country's inhabitants view entrepreneurs in terms of status and career choice and how the level of corruption in that country affects this view. Without strong cultural support, the best and brightest do not want to be responsible entrepreneurs, and they decide to enter a traditional profession. Career Status is the average percentage of the population age 18–64 who say that entrepreneurship is a good career choice and enjoys high status. The associated institutional variable measures the level of corruption. High levels of corruption can undermine the high status and steady career paths of legitimate entrepreneurs.[8]

Entrepreneurial Abilities Pillars

Pillar 6 *Opportunity Startup.* This is a measure of startups by people who are motivated by opportunity but face red tape and tax payment. An entrepreneur's motivation for starting a business is an important signal of quality. Opportunity entrepreneurs are believed to be better prepared, to have superior skills, and to earn more than what we call necessity entrepreneurs. Opportunity Motivation is defined as the percentage of the Total Entrepreneurial Activity (TEA) businesses started to exploit a good opportunity, to increase income, or to fulfill personal aims, in contrast to those started by people who have no other options for work. The overall effectiveness of

[6] Caliendo, Fossen, and Kritikos (2009), Vieider, Lefebvre, Bouchouicha, Chmura, Hakimov, and Krawczyk (2015).

[7] Shane and Cable (2003), Mian and Hattab (2013), Audretsch, Heger, and Veith (2015).

[8] Lee et al. (2011), Dutta and Sobel (2016).

the government services is measured by the Good Governance variable, and the cost of the governance is by the level of overall taxation (Taxation). The variable is a combination of these two components, government service quality and costs.[9]

Pillar 7 *Technology Absorption.* In the modern knowledge economy, information and communication technologies (ICT) play a crucial role in economic development. Not all sectors provide the same chances for businesses to survive and/or their potential for growth. The Technology Level variable is a measure of the businesses that are in technology sectors. The institutional variable, Tech Absorption, is a measure of a country's capacity for firm-level technology absorption, as reported by the World Economic Forum. The diffusion of new technology, and the capability to absorb it, is vital for innovative firms with high growth potential.[10]

Pillar 8 *Human Capital.* The prevalence of high-quality human capital is vitally important for ventures that are highly innovative and require an educated, experienced, and healthy workforce to continue to grow. An important feature of a venture with high growth potential is the entrepreneur's level of education. The Educational Level variable captures the quality of entrepreneurs; it is widely held that entrepreneurs with higher education degrees are more capable and willing to start and manage high-growth businesses. The labor market possibilities and the capability to easily hire quality employees also have an impact on business development, innovation, and growth potential. The institutional variable Labor Market has two components. Labor Freedom measures the freedom of the labor from the regulatory perspective and Staff Training is a country's level of investment in business training and employee development. It can be expected that heavy investment in employees pays off and that training increases employee quality.[11]

Pillar 9 *Competition.* Competition is a measure of a business's product or market uniqueness, combined with the market power of existing businesses and business groups and the effectiveness of anti-monopoly regulation. The variable Competitors is defined as the percentage of TEA businesses that have only a few competitors offering the same product or service. However, market entry can be prevented or made more difficult if powerful business groups are dominating the market. The extent of market dominance by a few business groups is measured by the variable Market Dominance, a variable reported by the World Economic Forum. The effectiveness of the regulatory bodies (Regulation) could also influence the level of competition in a country. The Competition institutional variable is the combination of Regulation and Market Dominance.[12]

---

[9] Asoni and Sanandaji (2014), Belitski, Chowdhury, and Desai (2016).

[10] Coad and Rao (2008), García-Morales, Bolívar-Ramos, and Martín-Rojas (2014).

[11] Bates (1990), Qian (2016).

[12] Baumol, Litan, and Schramm (2007), Calcagno and Sobel (2014).

Entrepreneurial Aspirations Pillars

Pillar 10 *Product Innovation.* New products play a crucial role in the economy of all countries. While countries were once the source of most new products, today developing countries are producing products that are dramatically cheaper than their Western equivalents. New Product is a measure of a country's potential to generate new products and to adopt or imitate existing products. In order to quantify the potential for new product innovation, an institutional variable related to technology and innovation transfer seems to be relevant. Technology Transfer is a complex measure of whether a business environment allows the application of innovations for developing new products.[13]

Pillar 11 *Process Innovation.* Applying and/or creating new technology is another important feature of businesses with high growth potential. New Tech is defined as the percentage of businesses whose principal underlying technology is less than five years old. However, most entrepreneurial businesses do not just apply new technology, they create it. The problem is similar to the New Product variable: whereas many businesses in developing countries may apply the latest technology, they tend to buy or copy it. An appropriate institutional variable applied here is complex measure combining research and development (R&D), the quality of scientific institutions in a country (Scientific Institutions) and the availability of scientists and engineers (Availability of Scientist). Gross Domestic Expenditure on Research and Development (GERD) is the R&D percentage of GDP as reported by OECD. While R&D alone does not guarantee successful growth, it is clear that, without systematic research activity, the development and the implementation of new technologies—and therefore future growth—will be inhibited. The Science institutional variable combines together R&D potential with physical scientific infrastructure and science oriented human capital.[14]

Pillar 12 *High Growth.* High Growth is a combined measure of the percentage of high-growth businesses that intend to employ at least 10 people and plan to grow more than 50 percent in five years (Gazelle variable) with business strategy sophistication (Business Strategy variable) and venture capital financing possibility (Venture Capital). It might be argued that a shortcoming of the Gazelle variable is that growth is not an actual but an expected rate. However, a measure of expected growth is in fact a more appropriate measure of aspiration than a measure of realized growth. Business Strategy refers to "the ability of companies to pursue distinctive strategies, which involves differentiated positioning and innovative means of production and service delivery." High Growth combines high growth potential with a sophisticated strategy and growth-specific venture capital finance.[15]

---

[13] Autio, Kenney, Mustar, Siegel, and Wright (2014).

[14] Stam and Wennberg (2009).

[15] Acs, Parsons, and Tracy (2008), Gompers and Lerner (2004).

Pillar 13 *Internationalization.* Internationalization is believed to be a major determinant of growth. A widely applied proxy for internationalization is exporting. Exporting demands capabilities beyond those needed by businesses that produce only for domestic markets. However, the institutional dimension is also important; a country's openness to international entrepreneurs—that is, the potential for internationalization—can be estimated by its degree of complexity." The complexity of an economy is related to the multiplicity of useful knowledge embedded in it. Because individuals are limited in what they know, the only way societies can expand their knowledge base is by facilitating the interaction of individuals in increasingly complex networks in order to make products. We can measure economic complexity by the mix of these products that countries are able to make." The internationalization pillar is designed to capture the degree to which a country's entrepreneurs are internationalized, as measured by the exporting potential of businesses, controlling for the extent to which the country is able to produce complex products.[16]

Pillar 14 *Risk Capital.* The availability of risk finance, particularly equity rather than debt, is an essential precondition for fulfilling entrepreneurial aspirations that are beyond an individual entrepreneur's personal financial resources.[17] Here we combine two kinds of finance, the informal investment (Informal Investment) and the institutional depth of capital market (DCM). Informal Investment is defined as the percentage of informal investors in the population age 18–64, multiplied by the average size of individuals' investment in other people's new businesses. While the rate of informal investment is high in factor-driven economies, the amount of informal investment is considerably larger in efficiency- and innovation-driven countries; combining them balances these two effects. Our institutional variable here is DCM, one of the six sub-indices of the Venture Capital and Private Equity Index. This variable is a complex measure of the size and liquidity of the stock market, level of IPO, M&A, and debt and credit market activity, which encompass seven aspects of a country's debt and capital market.

The Global Entrepreneurship and Development Index, 2017 Rankings

In this section, we report the rankings of the 137 countries on the Global Entrepreneurship and Development Index and its 3 sub-indices. We also provide confidence intervals for the GEI's. The confidence interval calculations are based on the Global Entrepreneurship Monitor (GEM) Total Early-Phased Entrepreneurial Activity (TEA) confidence intervals. Note that these confidence intervals only

[16] De Clercq, Sapienza, and Crijns (2005).

[17] Groh, Liechtenstein, and Lieser (2012a, 2012b).

partially represent the potential measurement errors, as we do not know the full error term. In addition, we do not have information about the confidence intervals of the 34 countries where we use estimated data. In these cases, the upper and the lower limits are the same.

We present the rankings in terms of country development, as measured by per capita GDP. The overall ranking of the countries on the GEI is shown in Table 3.1. Like previous years, Anglo-Saxon, Nordic, and Western European countries in the innovation-driven stage of development are in the front ranks. The United States, Switzerland, and Canada lead the rankings. The big surprise this year is the rise of Switzerland to the second place, primarily driven by the aspiration index with very strong scores in high-growth firms, product innovation, and process innovation. Three of the five Nordic countries, Denmark, Iceland, and Sweden, are in the top ten and effectively tied with the United States. Taiwan, the highest Asian country, is in 16th place, and Singapore is 24th, which virtually ties it with Japan. While the Netherlands rises to the 10th-place position just behind the United Kingdom that held its own in position. Besides their high entrepreneurial performance, these countries represent high-income levels.

Of the most populous EU countries, only the United Kingdom places eighth among the top ten countries. The other large European countries rank in the middle: Germany is 12th, France is 13th, and Spain is 32nd followed by Italy in 48th place. While the United Kingdom, France, and Germany are relatively well balanced over the 14 pillars, Poland, Spain, and Italy are entrepreneurially less efficient. A likely explanation for the EU countries' relatively weak economic performance over the last decade is their low level of entrepreneurship; the same applies to Japan, which took the 30th place. Europe is still struggling to create new billion-dollar companies.

Factor-driven countries with low GDPs, such as Pakistan, Bangladesh, Uganda, and other poor African countries, are at the bottom of the entrepreneurship ranking, as expected. At the same time, these countries' entrepreneurial performance is the least unbalanced. However, some countries—including two former socialist countries, Serbia and Russia, innovation-driven Italy, and two South American countries, Brazil and Trinidad and Tobago—should have higher levels of entrepreneurship, as implied by their development trend lines, and more efficient use of entrepreneurial resources.

The Ranking of the 3As

By definition, the GEI is a three-component index that takes into account the different aspects of the entrepreneurial ecosystem. However, all three components, called sub-indices, are in themselves complex measures that include various characteristics of entrepreneurial attitudes, entrepreneurial abilities, and entrepreneurial aspirations.

Table 3.1 The Global Entrepreneurship and Development Index Rank of All Countries, 2018

Global rank	Country	Score	Global rank	Country	Score	Global rank	Country	Score
1	United States	83.6	50	Hungary	36.4	96	Ecuador	20.5
2	Switzerland	80.4	51	Uruguay	35.0	97	Bolivia	20.4
3	Canada	79.2	52	Botswana	34.9	98	Brazil	20.3
4	United Kingdom	77.8	53	Brunei Darussalam	34.3	99	Tajikistan	20.0
5	Australia	75.5	54	Croatia	34.0	100	Kyrgyz Republic	19.8
6	Denmark	74.3	55	Barbados	33.6	101	Nigeria	19.7
7	Iceland	74.2	56	Costa Rica	33.3	102	Zambia	19.6
8	Ireland	73.7	57	South Africa	32.9	103	Senegal	19.2
9	Sweden	73.1	58	Malaysia	32.7	104	Libya	18.9
10	France	68.5	59	Lebanon	31.5	105	Côte d'Ivoire	18.9
11	Netherlands	68.1	60	Montenegro	31.2	106	Paraguay	18.7
12	Finland	67.9	61	Namibia	31.1	107	Honduras	18.7
13	Hong Kong	67.3	62	Azerbaijan	30.5	108	Guatemala	18.5
14	Austria	66.0	63	Belize	30.0	109	Kenya	18.4
15	Germany	65.9	64	Kazakhstan	29.7	110	Ethiopia	18.3
16	Israel	65.4	65	Morocco	29.2	111	Suriname	18.1
17	Belgium	63.7	66	Macedonia	29.1	112	Lao PDR	17.8
18	Taiwan	59.5	67	Peru	28.4	113	Cambodia	17.6
19	Chile	58.5	68	India	28.4	114	El Salvador	16.7
20	Luxembourg	58.2	69	Bulgaria	27.8	115	Tanzania	16.4
21	Norway	56.6	70	Panama	27.7	116	Guyana	16.4
22	Qatar	55.0	71	Thailand	27.4	117	Gambia. The	16.1
23	Estonia	54.8	72	Iran	26.8	118	Mali	15.9
24	Korea	54.2	73	Ukraine	26.8	119	Liberia	15.7
25	Slovenia	53.8	74	Serbia	26.4	120	Pakistan	15.6
26	United Arab Emirates	53.5	75	Mexico	26.4	121	Cameroon	15.4
27	Singapore	52.7	76	Egypt	25.9	122	Nicaragua	14.7
28	Japan	51.5	77	Georgia	25.8	123	Angola	14.4
29	Lithuania	51.1	78	Russia	25.2	124	Mozambique	14.0
30	Poland	50.4	79	Gabon	25.0	125	Madagascar	14.0
31	Portugal	48.8	80	Algeria	24.7	126	Venezuela	13.8
32	Cyprus	48.0	81	Trinidad & Tobago	24.4	127	Myanmar	13.6
33	Oman	46.9	82	Dominican Republic	24.3	128	Benin	13.3
34	Spain	45.3	83	Albania	24.2	129	Burkina Faso	13.2
35	Bahrain	45.1	84	Philippines	24.1	130	Guinea	12.9
36	Slovakia	44.9	85	Argentina	24.0	131	Uganda	12.9
37	Turkey	44.5	86	Swaziland	23.8	132	Sierra Leone	12.3

(continued)

Table 3.1 (continued)

Global rank	Country	Score	Global rank	Country	Score	Global rank	Country	Score
38	Czech Republic	43.4	87	Vietnam	23.2	133	Malawi	12.2
39	Kuwait	42.8	88	Armenia	22.8	134	Bangladesh	11.8
40	Tunisia	42.4	89	Jamaica	22.2	135	Burundi	11.8
41	Puerto Rico	42.1	90	Sri Lanka	21.9	136	Mauritania	10.9
42	Italy	41.4	91	Rwanda	21.5	137	Chad	9.0
43	China	41.1	92	Moldova	21.2			
44	Latvia	40.5	93	Ghana	21.0			
45	Saudi Arabia	40.2	94	Indonesia	20.7			
46	Romania	38.2	95	Bosnia and Herzegovina	20.7			
47	Colombia	38.2						
48	Greece	37.1						
49	Jordan	36.5						

Entrepreneurial attitudes are societies' attitudes toward entrepreneurship, which we define as a population's general feelings about recognizing opportunities, knowing entrepreneurs personally, endowing entrepreneurs with high status, accepting the risks associated with business startups, and having the skills to launch a business successfully. The benchmark individuals are those who can recognize valuable business opportunities and have the skills to exploit them, who attach high status to entrepreneurs, who can bear and handle startup risks, who know other entrepreneurs personally (i.e., have a network or role models), and who can generate future entrepreneurial activities.

Moreover, these people can provide the cultural support, financial resources, and networking potential to those who are already entrepreneurs or want to start a business. Entrepreneurial attitudes are important because they express the general feeling of the population toward entrepreneurs and entrepreneurship. Countries need people who can recognize valuable business opportunities and who perceive that they have the required skills to exploit these opportunities. Moreover, if national attitudes toward entrepreneurship are positive, it will generate cultural support, financial support, and networking benefits for those who want to start businesses.

Entrepreneurial abilities refer to the entrepreneurs' characteristics and those of their businesses. Different types of entrepreneurial abilities can be distinguished within the realm of new business efforts. Creating businesses may vary by industry sector, the legal form of organization, and demographics—age, education, etc. We define entrepreneurial abilities as startups in the medium- or high-technology sectors that are initiated by educated entrepreneurs and launched because of a person being motivated by an opportunity in an environment that is not overly competitive. In order to calculate the opportunity startup rate, we use the GEM TEA Opportunity Index. TEA captures new startups not only as the creation of new ventures but also as startups within existing businesses, such as a spin-off or other entrepreneurial efforts. Differences in the quality of startups are quantified by the entrepreneur's education level—that is, if they have a postsecondary education—and the uniqueness of the product or service as measured by the level of competition. Moreover, it is generally maintained that opportunity motivation is a sign of better planning, a more sophisticated strategy, and higher growth expectations than "necessity" motivation in startups.

Entrepreneurial aspiration reflects the quality aspects of startups and new businesses. Some people just dislike their currently employment situation and want to be their own boss, while others want to create the next Microsoft. Entrepreneurial aspiration is defined as the early-stage entrepreneur's effort to introduce new products and/or services, develop new production processes, penetrate foreign markets, substantially increase their company's staff, and finance their business with formal and/or informal venture capital. Product and process innovation, internationalization, and high growth are considered the key characteristics of entrepreneurship. Here we added a finance variable to capture the informal and formal venture capital potential that is vital for innovative startups and high-growth firms.

Each of these three building blocks of entrepreneurship influences the other two. For example, entrepreneurial attitudes influence entrepreneurial abilities and entrepreneurial aspirations, while entrepreneurial aspirations and abilities also influence entrepreneurial attitudes.

Table 3.2 shows the ranking of the first 25 countries in the GEI and the rank of the sub-index. The sub-index points and rankings for all 137 countries can be found in the Appendix. The United States is the first in the overall index and also in one out of the three sub-indices. Switzerland is eleventh in attitudes, second in aspirations, and third in abilities, as it is more interested in high-impact entrepreneurship than in replicative activities. Chile represents a more unbalanced case, ranking 18th in the overall index slipping three places, 8th in attitudes, 29th in abilities, and 27th in aspirations. This is a huge challenge for Chile and many other Latin American economies. Generally, countries that rank at the bottom of the GEI also rank at the bottom of the three sub-indices. Israel ranks 21st in the overall index but performs poorly in attitudes and abilities. However, it ranks 10th in aspirations, despite having poorer attitudes and abilities. For the "startup nation," it has an overall poor ranking in startup skills—at the bottom of the top 25 countries.

Tables 3.3, 3.4, and 3.5 list the ranks and the 14 pillar values of the first 25 countries for the 3 sub-indices. Each table gives the values for each of the pillars that make up the respective sub-index. The ranks and the pillar values for all 137 countries can be found in the Appendices.

Entrepreneurial Attitudes

As stated earlier, entrepreneurial attitude is defined as the general attitude of a country's population toward recognizing opportunities, knowing entrepreneurs personally, attaching high status to entrepreneurs, accepting the risks associated with a business startup, and having the skills to successfully launch businesses. Entrepreneurial attitudes are important because they express the population's general feelings toward entrepreneurs and entrepreneurship.

The benchmark individuals are those who can (1) recognize valuable business opportunities, (2) have the necessary skills to exploit these opportunities, (3) attach high status to and respect entrepreneurs, (4) handle startup risk, and (5) know entrepreneurs personally (i.e., have a network or role models). Moreover, these people can provide the cultural support, financial resources, and networking potential to those who are already entrepreneurs or want to start a business. Iceland leads in the Attitudes sub-index, followed by the United States, Finland, the Netherlands, Sweden, Canada, Australia, Chile, Denmark, and the United Kingdom. Japan has the lowest attitudes toward entrepreneurship as families do not encourage entrepreneurship for young people. Chile's eighth place is a very strong showing for a South American country. Factor-driven African and Asian countries, including Swaziland, Mali, Sierra Leone, Ethiopia, Bangladesh, Pakistan, Malawi, Chad, and Burundi, are at the bottom.

Table 3.2 The Global Entrepreneurship and Development Index and Sub-Index Ranks of the First 25 Countries, 2018

Countries	GEI	GEI rank	ATT	ATT rank	ABT	ABT rank	ASP	ASP rank
United States	83.6	1	80.0	2	86.0	2	84.9	2
Switzerland	80.4	2	69.5	11	86.4	1	85.5	1
Canada	79.2	3	77.9	5	79.9	5	79.9	3
United Kingdom	77.8	4	73.6	7	83.3	4	76.3	4
Australia	75.5	5	79.2	3	76.0	8	71.2	8
Denmark	74.3	6	71.9	8	84.5	3	66.5	16
Iceland	74.2	7	82.3	1	69.9	9	70.3	9
Ireland	73.7	8	67.2	14	78.9	6	75.0	5
Sweden	73.1	9	71.1	9	78.7	7	69.5	13
France	68.5	10	61.4	17	69.7	10	74.4	6
Netherlands	68.1	11	77.4	6	65.3	14	61.7	22
Finland	67.9	12	79.0	4	62.9	16	61.8	21
Hong Kong	67.3	13	69.4	12	62.5	17	70.2	10
Austria	66.0	14	67.3	13	66.4	13	64.4	17
Germany	65.9	15	61.1	18	67.2	12	69.4	14
Israel	65.4	16	63.3	16	60.8	20	72.2	7
Belgium	63.7	17	53.8	23	67.8	11	69.5	12
Taiwan	59.5	18	54.0	22	54.8	24	69.6	11
Chile	58.5	19	70.3	10	50.9	27	54.3	30
Luxembourg	58.2	20	49.2	28	62.9	15	62.6	18
Norway	56.6	21	66.1	15	60.9	19	42.8	44
Qatar	55.0	22	48.4	29	54.5	25	62.2	19
Estonia	54.8	23	57.6	19	55.7	22	51.0	35
Korea	54.2	24	55.6	20	50.1	29	56.8	27
Slovenia	53.8	25	54.4	21	55.0	23	52.1	33

High entrepreneurial abilities are associated with startups in the medium- or high-technology sectors that are initiated by educated entrepreneurs and launched because of opportunity motivation in a not too competitive environment. Quality differences in startups are quantified by the motivation and education level of the entrepreneur and by the uniqueness of the product or service, as measured by the level of competition.

Entrepreneurial Abilities

Denmark ranks number one on the Entrepreneurial Abilities sub-index and has a very strong showing in Opportunity Startups. The United States ranks second and is relatively weak in Opportunity Startup and Technology Absorption. Switzerland is

Table 3.3 Entrepreneurial Attitudes Sub-Index and Pillar Values for the First 25 Countries, 2018[a]

Countries	ATT	Opportunity Perception	Startup Skills	Risk Acceptance	Networking	Cultural Support
Iceland	82.3	0.947	1.000	0.917	1.000	0.633
United States	80.0	0.864	1.000	0.969	0.569	0.816
Australia	79.2	0.947	1.000	0.717	0.698	0.782
Finland	79.0	0.954	0.986	0.782	0.833	0.885
Canada	77.9	0.981	0.795	0.708	0.626	0.975
Netherlands	77.4	0.898	0.887	0.877	0.800	1.000
United Kingdom	73.6	0.810	0.573	0.876	0.619	0.928
Denmark	71.9	1.000	0.690	0.748	0.634	0.918
Sweden	71.1	1.000	0.472	0.704	0.740	0.896
Chile	70.3	0.821	0.903	1.000	0.709	0.628
Switzerland	69.5	0.776	0.719	0.879	0.533	0.673
Hong Kong	69.4	1.000	0.581	0.610	1.000	0.680
Austria	67.3	0.780	0.953	0.672	0.552	0.683
Ireland	67.2	0.766	0.966	0.801	0.390	0.780
Norway	66.1	1.000	0.540	0.999	0.473	1.000
Israel	63.3	0.738	0.598	0.481	1.000	0.738
France	61.4	0.502	0.558	0.751	0.673	0.641
Germany	61.1	0.775	0.627	0.657	0.380	0.842
Estonia	57.6	0.896	0.800	0.622	0.493	0.563
Korea	55.6	0.457	0.774	0.905	0.765	0.272
Slovenia	54.4	0.349	1.000	0.843	0.331	0.504
Taiwan	54.0	0.517	0.526	0.587	0.644	0.580
Belgium	53.8	0.679	0.677	0.559	0.349	0.568
Saudi Arabia	53.6	0.611	0.933	0.436	1.000	0.477
Spain	51.3	0.407	0.807	0.692	0.640	0.339

[a]Pillar values are the normalized pillar scores and after the average pillar correction.

Table 3.4 Entrepreneurial Abilities Sub-Index and Pillar Values for the First 25 Countries, 2018[a]

Countries	ABT	Opportunity Startup	Technology Absorption	Human Capital	Competition
Switzerland	86.4	0.966	1.000	0.789	1.000
United States	86.0	0.849	0.814	1.000	1.000
Denmark	84.5	1.000	1.000	1.000	0.989
United Kingdom	83.3	0.925	1.000	0.742	0.848
Canada	79.9	0.999	0.779	0.912	0.676
Ireland	78.9	1.000	0.769	0.851	1.000
Sweden	78.7	0.976	0.946	0.644	0.869
Australia	76.0	0.871	0.780	0.950	0.567
Iceland	69.9	1.000	1.000	0.506	0.501
France	69.7	0.683	0.840	0.625	0.739
Belgium	67.8	0.543	0.852	0.778	0.850
Germany	67.2	0.759	0.863	0.482	0.848
Austria	66.4	0.808	0.941	0.399	0.761
Netherlands	65.3	0.935	0.835	0.365	0.786
Luxembourg	62.9	1.000	0.839	0.551	0.857
Finland	62.9	1.000	0.826	0.495	0.415
Hong Kong	62.5	0.800	0.643	0.894	0.381
Japan	61.1	0.588	0.902	0.983	0.594
Norway	60.9	1.000	0.752	0.419	0.671
Israel	60.8	0.647	1.000	0.811	0.317
Singapore	58.6	1.000	0.739	1.000	0.655
Estonia	55.7	0.635	0.773	0.540	0.606
Slovenia	55.0	0.604	0.744	0.500	0.485
Taiwan	54.8	0.651	0.705	0.701	0.317
Qatar	54.5	0.754	0.339	0.882	0.603

[a]Pillar values are the normalized pillar scores and after the average pillar correction.

stronger than the United States in two pillars, Opportunity Startups and Technology Absorption, but very weak in Human Capital. The United Kingdom ranks fourth, with a significantly lower Entrepreneurial Abilities score than Denmark, the United States and Switzerland. Sweden is strong in Opportunity Startup and Technology Absorption but low on Human Capital. The first four countries are followed by Ireland, Canada, Australia, Belgium, and Iceland.

Entrepreneurial Aspirations

Entrepreneurial aspiration is the early-stage entrepreneur's effort to introduce new products and/or services, develop new production processes, penetrate foreign markets, substantially increase the firm's staff, and finance a business with formal

Table 3.5 Entrepreneurial Aspirations Sub-Index and Pillar Values for the First 25 Countries, 2018[a]

Countries	ASP	Product Innovation	Process Innovation	High Growth	Internationalization	Risk Capital
Switzerland	85.5	0.834	0.902	0.882	1.000	1.000
United States	84.9	0.733	0.902	1.000	1.000	0.876
Canada	79.9	0.991	0.758	0.559	0.936	1.000
United Kingdom	76.3	0.924	0.701	0.850	0.824	0.649
Ireland	75.0	1.000	0.822	0.884	0.970	0.568
France	74.4	0.801	0.941	0.644	0.764	0.768
Israel	72.2	0.997	1.000	0.851	0.601	0.788
Australia	71.2	0.592	0.786	0.658	0.633	1.000
Iceland	70.3	0.602	0.838	0.699	0.952	0.588
Hong Kong	70.2	0.884	0.409	1.000	0.679	1.000
Taiwan	69.6	0.972	0.696	0.895	0.536	0.935
Belgium	69.5	0.913	0.963	0.551	0.887	0.627
Sweden	69.5	0.666	0.899	0.557	0.816	0.721
Germany	69.4	0.667	0.840	0.662	0.874	0.760
United Arab Emirates	68.1	1.000	0.626	0.899	0.901	0.979
Denmark	66.5	0.988	0.723	0.594	0.390	1.000
Austria	64.4	0.724	0.818	0.403	0.901	0.630
Luxembourg	62.6	1.000	0.612	0.545	1.000	0.902
Qatar	62.2	0.856	0.516	1.000	0.529	0.956
Japan	62.1	0.788	1.000	1.000	0.606	0.547
Finland	61.8	0.617	0.795	0.675	0.647	0.497
Netherlands	61.7	0.652	0.769	0.596	0.562	0.715
Singapore	61.6	0.763	1.000	1.000	1.000	0.796
China	60.0	1.000	0.759	0.871	0.310	1.000
Lithuania	59.2	0.708	0.502	0.636	0.736	0.641

[a]Pillar values are the normalized pillar scores after the average pillar correction.

and/or informal venture capital. In other words, the effort to start new companies that will generate wealth and can be scaled. Product and process innovation, internationalization, and high growth are considered characteristics of entrepreneurship. The benchmark entrepreneurs are those whose businesses (1) produce and sell products/services considered to be new to at least some customers, (2) use a technology less than 5 years old, (3) have sales in foreign markets, (4) plan to employ at least ten people, and (5) have greater than 50 percent growth over the next 5 years. The Finance variable captures the informal venture capital potential, as well as the development of capital, venture capital, and credit markets, which is vital for innovative startups and high-growth firms.

The United States leads in the Entrepreneurial Aspirations sub-index. While showing some weakness in Product and Process Innovation, it is very strong in High

Growth, Internationalization, and Risk Capital. Switzerland is second, showing strength in Internationalization and Risk Capital, followed by Canada, Taiwan, Sweden, Ireland, Australia, Iceland, and Germany, which round out the top ten.

Summaries and Conclusion

Entrepreneurship is similar to other social creatures, in that it is a multidimensional phenomenon whose exact meaning is difficult to identify. There is only one thing more difficult: how to measure this vaguely defined creature. Over the decades, researchers have created several entrepreneurship indicators, but none has been able to reflect the complex nature of entrepreneurship and provide a plausible explanation of its role in development. The Global Entrepreneurship and Development Index is the first, and presently the only, complex measure of the national-level entrepreneurship ecosystem that reflects the multifaceted nature of entrepreneurship. In this chapter, we presented the entrepreneurial performance of 137 of the world's countries, which included country-level values for the GEI—entrepreneurial attitudes, entrepreneurial abilities, and entrepreneurial aspirations—and for the 14 pillars.

References

Acs, Z. J., Parsons, W., & Tracy, S. (2008). *High impact firms: Gazelles revisited* (Office of Advocacy working paper, U.S. Small Business Administration), http://www.sba.gov/advocacy/847/17231.

Asoni, A., & Sanandaji, T. (2014). Taxation and the quality of entrepreneurship. *Journal of Economics, 113*(2), 101–123.

Audretsch, D. B., Heger, D., & Veith, T. (2015). Infrastructure and entrepreneurship. *Small Business Economics, 44*(2), 219–230.

Autio, E., Kenney, M., Mustar, P., Siegel, D., & Wright, M. (2014). Entrepreneurial innovation: The importance of context. *Research Policy, 43*(7), 1097–1108.

Bates, T. (1990). Entrepreneur human capital inputs and small business longevity. *The Review of Economics and Statistics, 72*, 551–559.

Baumol, W. (1990). Entrepreneurship: Productive, unproductive and destructive. *Journal of Political Economy, 98*, 893–921.

Baumol, W., Litan, R., & Schramm, C. (2007). *Good capitalism, bad capitalism, and the economics of growth and prosperity*. New Haven, CT: Yale University Press.

Belitski, M., Chowdhury, F., & Desai, S. (2016). Taxes, corruption, and entry. *Small Business Economics, 47*(1), 201–216.

Bhola, R., Verheul, I., Thurik, R., & Grilo, I. (2006). *Explaining engagement levels of opportunity and necessity entrepreneurs (EIM working paper series H200610)*. Netherlands: Zoetermeer.

Bjørnskov, C., & Foss, N. (2010). Economic freedom and entrepreneurial activity: Some cross-country evidence. In *Entrepreneurship and Culture* (pp. 201–225). Berlin Heidelberg: Springer.

Calcagno, P. T., & Sobel, R. S. (2014). Regulatory costs on entrepreneurship and establishment employment size. *Small Business Economics, 42*(3), 541–559.

Caliendo, M., Fossen, F. M., & Kritikos, A. S. (2009). Risk attitudes of nascent entrepreneurs: New evidence from an experimentally validated survey. *Small Business Economics, 32*, 153–167.

Coad, A., & Rao, R. (2008). Innovation and firm growth in "complex technology" sectors: A quantile regression approach. *Research Policy, 37*, 633–648.

Davidsson, P. (2004). *Researching entrepreneurship*. New York: Springer.

De Clercq, D., Sapienza, H. J., & Crijns, H. (2005). The internationalization of small and medium firms. *Small Business Economics, 24*, 409–419.

Dutta, D. K., Li, J., & Merenda, M. (2011). Fostering entrepreneurship: impact of specialization and diversity in education. *International Entrepreneurship and Management Journal, 7*(2), 163–179.

Dutta, N., & Sobel, R. (2016). Does corruption ever help entrepreneurship. *Small Business Economics, 47*(1), 179–199.

García-Morales, V. J., Bolívar-Ramos, M. T., & Martín-Rojas, R. (2014). Technological variables and absorptive capacity's influence on performance through corporate entrepreneurship. *Journal of Business Research, 67*(7), 1468–1477.

Gartner, W. B. (1990). What are we talking about when we talk about entrepreneurship. *Journal of Business Venturing, 5*(1), 15–28.

Godin, K., Clemens, J., & Veldhuis, N. (2008). Measuring entrepreneurship conceptual frameworks and empirical indicators. *Studies in Entrepreneurship Markets, 7*, 28–40.

Goel, R. K., Nelson, M. A., & Payne, J. E. (2015). Entrepreneurship and cross-national economic freedom. In R. J. Cebula, C. Hall, F. G. Mixon Jr., & J. E. Payne (Eds.), *Economic behavior, economic freedom, and entrepreneurship* (pp. 222–235). Cheltenham: Edward Elgar Publishing.

Gompers, P., & Lerner, J. (2004). *The venture capital cycle*. Cambridge, MA: MIT Press.

Groh, A., Liechtenstein, H., & Lieser, K. (2012a). *The global venture capital and private equity country attractiveness index, 2012*.

Groh, A., Liechtenstein, H., & Lieser, K. (2012b). *The global venture capital and private equity country attractiveness index*.http://blog.iese.edu/vcpeindex/about/.

Gupta, V., & Gupta, A. (2015). The concept of entrepreneurial orientation. *Foundations and Trends (R) in Entrepreneurship, 11*(2), 55–137.

Ibrahim, N., & Mas'ud, A. (2016). Moderating role of entrepreneurial orientation on the relationship between entrepreneurial skills, environmental factors and entrepreneurial intention: A PLS approach. *Management Science Letters, 6*(3), 225–236.

Lee, S. M., Lim, S. B., & Pathak, R. D. (2011). Culture and entrepreneurial orientation: a multicountry study. *International Entrepreneurship and Management Journal, 7*(1), 1–15.

Mian, S. A., & Hattab, H. W. (2013). How individual competencies shape the entrepreneur's social network structure: evidence from the MENA region. *International Journal of Business and Globalisation, 11*(4), 399–412.

Papagiannidis, S., & Li, F. (2005). Skills brokerage: A new model for business startups in the networked economy. *European Management Journal, 23*, 471–482.

Qian, H. (2016). Skills and knowledge-based entrepreneurship: evidence from US cities. *Regional Studies, 43*, 1–14.

Shane, S., & Cable, D. (2003). Network ties, reputation, and the financing of new ventures. *Management Science, 48*, 364–381.

Stam, E., & Wennberg, K. (2009). The roles of R&D in new firm growth. *Small Business Economics, 33*(1), 77–89.

Thurik, A. R., Stam, E., & Audretsch, D. B. (2013). The rise of the entrepreneurial economy and the future of dynamic capitalism. *Technovation, 33*(8), 302–310.

Tumasjan, A., & Braun, R. (2012). In the eye of the beholder: How regulatory focus and self-efficacy interact in influencing opportunity recognition. *Journal of Business Venturing, 27*(6), 622–636.

Vieider, F. M., Lefebvre, M., Bouchouicha, R., Chmura, T., Hakimov, R., Krawczyk, M., et al. (2015). Common components of risk and uncertainty attitudes across contexts and domains: Evidence from 30 countries. *Journal of the European Economic Association, 13*(3), 421–452.

Vivarelli, M. (2013). Is entrepreneurship necessarily good? Microeconomic evidence from developed and developing countries. *Industrial and Corporate Change, 22*(6), 1453–1495.

Wennekers, S., & Thurik, R. (1999). Linking entrepreneurship to economic growth. *Small Business Economics, 13*(1), 27–55.

Zahra, S. A., Wright, M., & Abdelgawad, S. G. (2014). Contextualization and the advancement of entrepreneurship research. *International Small Business Journal*, 026624261351980.

Chapter 4
Enhancing Countries' Productivity Through a Healthy Entrepreneurial Ecosystem

Introduction

As a national phenomenon, entrepreneurship is much more than the mere rate of new businesses or self-employment rates. Within a territorial context, any definition of entrepreneurship should take into consideration the interconnectedness between individual actions and the institutional setting backing entrepreneurial actions which, ultimately, fuel the economy by creating jobs and development. This argument is not new, and support policies—for example, tax incentives and subsidies—tend to excessively focus on how to quickly increase self-employment rates, in an effort to generate outcomes that cater to the short-term tastes of policymakers. Nevertheless, higher government spending on private subsidies does not necessarily yield the desired entrepreneurial outcomes.[1]

Besides the definitional element, a second aspect of interest relates to the differentiating effect of entrepreneurship on country-level performance. Much has been said on the relationship between ambiguous entrepreneurship measures—such as the TEA—and economic development or growth, in terms of variations in GDP. But in this chapter we emphasize the value of distinguishing economic growth—the increase in the country's GDP, that is, "do more"—from productivity, that is, learn how to better exploit available resources.

The Global Entrepreneurship and Development Index constitutes a tool that helps conceptualize and measure the entrepreneurial ecosystem of countries and to better understand the economic repercussions of a healthy entrepreneurship ecosystem. Here, we propose to disentangle total factor productivity in two components that are economically relevant for the different stakeholders within any society:

1. The productivity effect: "do things better".
2. The innovation effect: "create new things or find new ways to do things".

---

[1]Acs Z., and P. Correa. The World Bank and GEDI, Identifying the Obstacles to High-Impact Entrepreneurship in Latin America and the Caribbean, (2014).

Z. J. Ács et al., *Global Entrepreneurship and Development Index 2018*, SpringerBriefs in Economics, https://doi.org/10.1007/978-3-030-03279-1_4

Country-Level Productivity and the Entrepreneurial Ecosystem

Perhaps the first point that should be made in this chapter is that economic growth does not equal to productivity. Economic growth basically refers to the capacity of countries to produce more goods and services, irrespective of how higher production is achieved. The positive variations in GDP or employment over time are the usual suspects among those interested in studying economic growth figures, mostly because they represent the desired objective of most policymakers, as a measure of economic prosperity.

Productivity is a more complex concept. At the country level, total factor productivity (TFP) deals with two highly interconnected economic aspects. First, TFP has to do with the capacity of countries to allocate and exploit available resources efficiently (P = productivity effect). The notion that markets are good at directing resources is a good catchall explanation concept; but for many businesses it is hard to find all that is required to perform in the market and to keep the pace of industrial and digital revolutions that not only equip businesses with new—often more technologically advanced—resources but also change the ways to exploit them. Contrary to the case of many small- and medium-sized retailers, large companies—including Walmart, Pier1, or H&M—have been criticized for their slowness to embrace digital shopping, that is, for their lack of capacity to introduce new technological recourses that will likely rise (even more!) their customer pie.[1] Without judging the profitability of e-commerce, the success of businesses is strictly linked to their capacity to exploit all resources available in the market.

The second component of TFP deal with the capacity of organizations to channel innovations to the economy (I = innovation effect) that, consequently, translate into higher levels of output per input unit (in the case of countries, GDP per worker). Maybe we all are too used to link innovation to technological inventions that are successfully commercialized. However, our definition of innovation is not restricted to engineering (such as the driverless car) or to medical advances (such as nerve stimulation or noninvasive procedures) and is open to other, equally valuable, types of non-technological innovations related to product and processes.

For example, Starbucks was founded in 1971 by a teacher (Gerald Baldwin), a writer (Gordon Bowker), and a historian (Zev Siegl). Starbucks basically serves coffee; but the company introduced an innovative coffee shop experience that has caught the eye of millions around the world. That is a case of a successful product innovation process developed by non-technological entrepreneurs. Zara, a Spanish chain of clothing retail shops founded in 1974 by Amancio Ortega (formerly a shop man and cloth maker), sells clothes and accessories (even the Cro-Magnon man learnt to make clothing!). But, Zara (part of the Inditex Corp.) is a good example of non-tech process innovation. To maximize the concept of fast fashion—the movement of designs from catwalk to the store in the fastest time—the company introduced modifications in the value chain. These changes mostly become evident in short periods of collection manufacturing (takes 2 weeks from market research to the market!) and in the enhanced information systems adopted by the company that collects and processes valuable fashion information from end customers. We can put many other examples (Cirque du Soleil, Facebook, Uber), and the conclusion will be the same: these companies did not invent any technology; they just invented a new way to do things better. The efforts of low-tech entrepreneurship do contribute to the economy by expanding its production possibilities.

In plain words, the combined effects of productivity and innovation shape total factor productivity (TFP = $P * I$). However, the capacity of countries to produce GDP is bounded by their available resources and their transformative capabilities. This way, total factor productivity defines the countries' production frontier and captures productivity variations that originate in differences in both production factors (P) and technology linked to innovation activities (I).[1]

Underlying this definition of productivity are two clearly differentiated effects. For illustrative purposes, Fig. 4.1 graphically presents the countries' production frontier in two periods, as well as the productivity and innovation effects.

Let's start with the productivity effect (P). The efficient allocation of resources available in the economy is an important part of the productivity function. The productivity effect is linked to how well new and existing businesses use different resources, including labor, capital, equipment, knowledge, and technology-based inputs. The capacity of Amazon to amalgamate technologies brought from other industries (e.g., ICTs, drones) to increase the productivity of its operations (delivery: AmazonFresh or Amazon Prime Air) is a good example.[1]

From the perspective of the entrepreneurship ecosystem, better institutions backing entrepreneurial activities and an efficient interaction between individual actions and the institutional setting governing entrepreneurial decisions are key ingredients necessary to facilitate the creation of businesses with a greater capacity to generate jobs and help incumbent businesses to take advantage of better market conditions. For example, in many European countries, entrepreneurs have strong incentives to invest in physical and human capital and to promote the exploitation of resources in an effort to improve the functioning of their businesses. In this case,

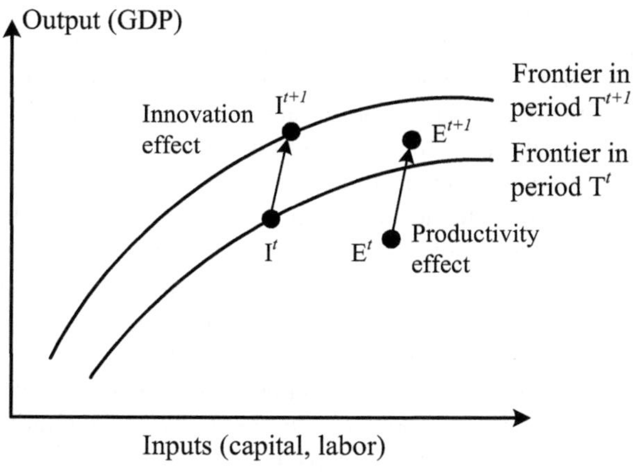

Fig. 4.1 Sources of total factor productivity

the supportive institutional environment creates the conditions to promote operational improvements. In other words, entrepreneurial ventures have incentives to "do things better," that is, to improve their productivity. To sum up, a healthy entrepreneurial ecosystem contributes to the national productivity by enhancing market efficiency levels and by promoting the efficient exploitation of resources through new and incumbent businesses.[1]

If we aggregate all the efforts by new and incumbent businesses to "do things better," it is possible to obtain the national outcomes carried out by these agents. These productive efforts will translate in a more efficient allocation and exploitation of resources that will move the country closer to the maximum potential level of GDP that it can produce, that is, closer to the production frontier, irrespective of the quality of production factors. On contrary, if businesses in the economy (new and incumbent) do not combine efficiently their resources, the country will be below the production possibility frontier.

Graphically, this is the case of the fictitious country "E" in Fig. 4.1. In the example, country "E" is off the global frontier in the two periods proposed in the example (T^t and T^{t+1}). The country can improve the allocation of resources among new and existing businesses by enhancing the quality of its entrepreneurial ecosystem, and this will lead to productivity effects. In the example, the entrepreneurial ecosystem of country "E" helps to channel entrepreneurial resources to the economy and achieve a greater GDP level in the second period (T^{t+1}), compared to the first one (T^t). In this case, the productivity effect (*P*) becomes evident in the observed improvement in the position of the country with respect to the production frontier.

The second effect—innovation (*I*)—is strictly linked to the Schumpeterian approach to entrepreneurship (creative destruction).[1] For Schumpeter entrepreneurs play a decisive role in the economy by creating and implementing radical innovations that are conducive to economic progress. In this tradition entrepreneurship is critical to spark economic development by promoting innovations, in our terminology "create new things or find new ways to do things." Following Fig. 4.1, progress translates in the expansion of the countries' production possibilities that materializes in a shift of the global frontier.

But, at this point is worth questioning how can radical innovations foster such progress. Moreover, how does the entrepreneurial ecosystem contribute to this progress? It seems logical to argue that inventions are worthless if they do not turn into commercialized innovations and that the economic impact of such innovations will turn sterile if the market and individuals cannot fully incorporate these innovations in their day-to-day routines.

For example, according to the World Bank,[1] the deepening of the cellular technology has rapidly grown in most countries, and smartphones are easily accessible today, regardless of the stage of development of the country. Nevertheless, the use of this technology in developing countries—for example, in Africa—is hampered both by the lack of education on how to use ICTs and by the limited capacity of these economies to create support structures that help optimize the use of technological devices or tools (e.g., access to 2G–4G technologies, applications, cell tower networks, or bandwidth capacity).[1]

On contrary, in the United States, the dynamics of private institutions—for example, universities and research centers—and the characteristics of capital markets, both essential elements of a healthy entrepreneurial ecosystem, give entrepreneurs the incentives to invest in physical and human capital and to promote the development and commercialization of innovations that contribute to improve the functioning of organizations. In this case, the supportive institutional environment provides entrepreneurs the mechanisms to generate and disseminate knowledge that triggers effective innovative entrepreneurship with economic potential, that is, the innovation effect.

For Schumpeter, entrepreneurs nurture the economy with innovations, and the entrepreneurial ecosystem is critical for the development of this economic function: "create new things or find new ways to do things." If countries enjoy a healthy entrepreneurial ecosystem, the efforts of innovative entrepreneurs will materialize in new value-adding combinations of resources that will expand the countries' productive capacity and the global production frontier.

Perhaps a brief analysis of patent grants around the globe constitutes a good case to exemplify how the entrepreneurial ecosystem contributes to the effective development of innovations. A patent is an exclusive right granted for an invention, which is a product or a process that provides, in general, a new way of doing something or offers a new technical solution to a problem. Patent count is a measurement of innovation commonly used by policymakers and scholars and points to the amount of resources a company is willing to put into its research as well as into its in-house patent team.

Obviously, businesses will invest in innovation only if they have access to the human capital, financial resources, as well as infrastructures necessary to create and commercialize their inventions. For example, IBM spent around $5.4 billion in 2016 on research and development, racking up a record number of 8088 patents awarded in 2016 developed by more than 8500 inventors working at the business.[1]

Moreover, IBM issued 7355 patents in 2015, and this number almost equals to the total number of patents issued by all African countries (8500) in 2015, according to the World Intellectual Property Organization (WIPO: www.wipo.int/ipstats/en/). This result is not surprising if we consider that the entrepreneurial ecosystem of African countries (average GEI = 19.31) does not offer businesses (new and incumbent) an environment that promotes the development of innovations and guarantees the commercialization and marketability of business innovations.

Additional data made available by WIPO reveal that the total patent grants registered by Chinese businesses skyrocketed between 2010 (135,110) and 2015 (359,316). Among US and European businesses, which operate in contexts with a more supportive entrepreneurial ecosystem, R&D investments by new and incumbent businesses is on top spots of the ranking, although patenting grew at a slower pace in these economies. US businesses issued 219,614 patents in 2010 and 298,407 in 2015, while European businesses issued a total number of 160,800 patents in 2010 and 165,400 in 2015.[1]

To summarize, the innovation effect (*I*) will materialize in superior total factor productivity in economies where the entrepreneurial ecosystem is strong enough to favor and promote the creation and commercialization of inventions and where the economic potential of such innovative entrepreneurship triggers changes in the countries' production function that shift the production frontier. For example, let's suppose the case of the fictitious country "*I*" in Fig. 4.1. In this case, country "*I*" is at the vanguard of technology and is positioned on the global frontier in the two periods proposed in the example (T^t and T^{t+1}). This country, which can perfectly be the United States, enjoys the policies (e.g., the Bayh-Dole Act of 1980)[1] and the market mechanisms to sway entrepreneurs toward a pathway of innovation seeking to channel value-adding innovations to the market that expand the country's production capacity. This innovation effect will become evident in the shift of the country's production frontier in subsequent time periods (T^{t+1}), relative to that in previous periods (T^t).

Total Factor Productivity Around the Globe: The Relevance of Entrepreneurial Ecosystems

So far, we have argued that entrepreneurship impacts total factor productivity (TFP) via two differentiating effects (TFP = $P * I$): productivity (P) and innovation (I). This suggests that a superior entrepreneurial ecosystem does not necessarily make a country richer but, rather, shapes economic and market structures as well as cultural aspects of societies, all important factors of the entrepreneurial ecosystem that improve total factor productivity.

We first explored the relationship between the GEI index and total factor productivity (TFP), paying special attention to the productivity (P) and innovation (I) effects. To do this we used data made available by the International Monetary Fund (IMF) to compute, for each country, the total factor productivity values (TFP = $P * I$)—defined as the capacity to produce GDP (output) using the capital stock and the labor force as inputs—as well as the productivity (P = use resources more efficiently) and the innovation (I = do new things to shift the production frontier) effects.[1]

We found a significant, relatively strong positive correlation between entrepreneurship and total factor productivity (0.35). We also noted that entrepreneurship correlates weakly positively with the productivity effect (0.09) (Table 4.1).

The strongest positive correlation was found between entrepreneurship and the innovation effect (0.39). This result is not surprising if we think a little harder. Just like we cannot imagine progress in the nineteenth century without the creation and development of steam engines, it is hard to imagine entrepreneurship in the twenty-first century without the power of technology-driven inventions. With the new millennium, industries and markets from all around the globe are witnessing drastic transformations that are the result of a digital revolution in which entrepreneurs are taking an active role by creating new businesses that are responsible of this revolution. The result is a good sign that reinforces our argument that the creation of "new things or new ways to do things" definitely constitutes the vital force driving economic development.

Table 4.1 The correlations between GEI, total factor productivity, and its components

Variables	Correlation
GEI vs. total factor productivity	0.35
GEI vs. productivity effect	0.09
GEI vs. innovation effect	0.39

The next question we explored is: Does the quality of the entrepreneurial ecosystem improve total factor productivity? The results of the total factor productivity reveal that four countries are on the production frontier: Iran, Nigeria, Norway, and the United States. This only means that these economies are producing their maximum possible GDP level using their available resources.

Clearly, countries such as Norway and the United States are usual suspects if we are looking for efficient territories. Norway and the United States not only are developed countries at the vanguard of innovation in different industry fields but also promote productive entrepreneurship by providing entrepreneurs with stable policies and a supportive entrepreneurial ecosystem.

Placing developing countries like Iran and Nigeria on the global frontier looks puzzling, but again if we think a little harder this makes sense. Productivity and the level of GDP cannot be treated as interchangeable terms. GDP growth only represents the answer to the question "is the country producing more?" The variation in total factor productivity is the observable outcome of countries' efforts for producing more with the same resources (productivity effect = "doing things better") and for successfully introducing new technologies (either generated inside or brought from outside) that expand the country's production capacity (innovation effect = "create new things or find new ways to do things").

So, although it looks counterintuitive, this result is consistent with the notion that productivity is compatible with differences in resource endowments across economies. In plain words, developing and undercapitalized countries like Iran and Nigeria are on the global production frontier because they know how to squeeze and exploit their scarce resources to get the most out of them. Norway and the United States are rock solid economies whose level and quality of productive inputs (e.g., financial resources, human capital) are out of the league of most developing economies. In the neighborhood of rich countries, Norway and the United States are on top and lead the global frontier. In the other side of the coin, countries like Iran and Nigeria make an efficient use of the limited resources, and they are the most productive economies in the neighborhood of underdeveloped and developing countries.[1]

This result is in line with our argument placed at the beginning of this subchapter: the entrepreneurial ecosystem does not make a country richer but, instead, gives entrepreneurs supportive economic and market structures as well as an appropriate environment, and all these elements are critical to achieve superior levels of total factor productivity.

But, how much does the entrepreneurial ecosystem contribute to countries' productivity? The computed values for total factor productivity, as well as for the productivity and innovation effects, are presented in Table 4.2. Note that, because of data availability from the IMF, the analysis limited to 63 countries for the period 2012–2013. Positive values are evidence of productivity improvements (TFP),

Table 4.2 Total factor productivity around the globe (TFP and its components)

Country	TFP	Productivity effect	Innovation effect	Country	TFP	Productivity effect	Innovation effect
Algeria	0.04%	1.72%	−1.65%	Latvia	3.19%	1.28%	1.89%
Angola	−4.03%	−3.45%	−0.60%	Lithuania	7.68%	4.06%	3.48%
Argentina	−0.38%	1.21%	−1.57%	Macedonia	−0.73%	−3.70%	3.08%
Barbados	1.37%	1.96%	−0.58%	Malawi	2.19%	1.53%	0.65%
Belgium	3.01%	1.54%	1.45%	Malaysia	1.91%	2.53%	−0.61%
Bosnia and Herzegovina	−0.82%	−0.49%	−0.33%	Mexico	1.44%	−1.87%	3.37%
Botswana	4.32%	5.11%	−0.75%	Namibia	−1.30%	−3.02%	1.77%
Brazil	2.75%	2.06%	0.68%	Netherlands	0.44%	−0.75%	1.20%
Canada	3.25%	1.49%	1.73%	Nigeria	−1.43%	0.00%	−1.43%
Chile	2.03%	1.41%	0.60%	Norway	2.39%	0.00%	2.39%
China	−3.97%	−7.42%	3.72%	Panama	4.27%	2.78%	1.45%
Colombia	−0.76%	−0.44%	−0.32%	Peru	−2.60%	−2.05%	−0.56%
Croatia	0.82%	−0.74%	1.57%	Poland	1.05%	2.01%	−0.94%
Czech Republic	0.85%	−1.62%	2.51%	Portugal	3.53%	0.92%	2.58%
Denmark	2.74%	0.92%	1.80%	Romania	5.73%	2.03%	3.63%
Ecuador	1.18%	−0.29%	1.47%	Russia	3.40%	2.03%	1.34%
Estonia	3.04%	1.08%	1.93%	Singapore	5.34%	2.32%	2.95%
Finland	3.56%	0.83%	2.72%	Slovakia	3.86%	1.77%	2.05%
France	0.59%	−0.43%	1.02%	Slovenia	1.93%	−0.04%	1.97%
Germany	1.05%	−0.74%	1.80%	South Africa	−0.06%	0.65%	−0.70%

Ghana	−2.85%	−3.97%	1.16%	Spain	−0.44%	−1.74%	1.32%
Greece	0.00%	−0.32%	0.32%	Sweden	0.56%	−0.63%	1.19%
Guatemala	2.07%	1.42%	0.65%	Switzerland	1.39%	−0.06%	1.45%
Hungary	3.90%	2.17%	1.69%	Thailand	4.73%	3.28%	1.40%
India	−2.67%	3.37%	−5.84%	Trinidad & Tobago	4.69%	4.97%	−0.27%
Iran	−0.51%	0.00%	−0.51%	Turkey	1.48%	2.12%	−0.62%
Ireland	1.57%	0.13%	1.45%	Uganda	−3.24%	−2.66%	−0.59%
Israel	0.94%	0.39%	0.55%	United Kingdom	3.25%	1.49%	1.73%
Italy	−0.27%	−1.00%	0.73%	United States	1.33%	0.00%	1.33%
Jamaica	−0.07%	0.33%	−0.40%	Uruguay	6.26%	1.16%	5.04%
Japan	2.80%	0.86%	1.93%	Zambia	−0.67%	−0.09%	−0.58%
Korea	1.13%	0.24%	0.89%				
Global average	**1.40%**	**0.44%**	**0.96%**				

efficiency improvements (*P* = productivity effect), and effective implementation of technologies (*I* = innovation effect). Negative values point to a decline in TFP, in the countries' productivity level (*P*), or in the innovation efficiency (*I*).

The data shows that, on average, countries improved their total factor productivity by 1.40%, and that most of the TFP improvement was caused by effective innovations (0.96%). The TFP improvement in the United States (1.33%) was entirely caused by effective implementation of innovations. That is, US businesses (new and incumbent) know very well how to capitalize on their vast amount of available resources so their productivity effect was null, and their major strength relies in their capacity to generate and channel innovations to the market. In the case of Europe, the increase in total factor productivity was the greatest (2.08%), and it is the result of mixed effects. On one hand, businesses in these economies are learning how to do things better (average productivity effect = 0.52%). On the other hand, and similar to the US, European businesses are benefiting from the quality of their entrepreneurial ecosystems to effectively implement innovations in markets (innovation effect = 1.56%).

On contrary, in Latin American and Asian economies, the observed increase in total factor productivity primarily comes from the productivity effect linked to the better use of resources by new and incumbent businesses. In the case of Latin America, businesses are learning how to better use their available resources, which translates in a productivity effect of 1.01%, while the innovation effect was 0.88%. Similarly, Asian economies mostly benefitted more from the exploitation of resources executed by businesses located in these countries (productivity effect = 0.81%), than from the implementation of innovations (innovation effect = 0.37%).

Finally, African businesses did not contribute to improve the total factor productivity of these economies. In fact, the average TFP level of these economies fell down by 1.04%, which is not surprising if we take into account that businesses in the countries operate in a context with a much less developed entrepreneurial ecosystem. Here, a positive innovation effect linked to the effective introduction of innovations was found only for Ghana, Malawi, and Namibia. The TFP loses in these economies were mostly caused by a poor exploitation of available resources. In other words, African businesses are doing less with the same resources, and that translates in a productivity decline (productivity effect = −1.03%).

These results somehow reflect the heterogeneity of the entrepreneurial ecosystem across economies. So, turning our attention to the question "how much does the entrepreneurial ecosystem contribute to countries' productivity?," the answer seems to be that there is a positive relationship between entrepreneurship and total factor productivity.

A first analysis in Table 4.3 shows that TFP grew more in innovation-driven economies that enjoy a healthy entrepreneurial ecosystem (1.98%), and this growth is mostly explained by the capacity of businesses in these economies for introducing value-adding innovations in the market (innovation effect = 1.55%). On contrary, in factor-driven countries with poor entrepreneurial ecosystems, total factor productivity fell down 0.34%, mainly because businesses in these economies are doing things worst, even with new technologies (either generated inside or brought from outside

Table 4.3 The correlations between GEI, total factor productivity, and its components in underdeveloped, developing, and developed economies

Variables	GEI	TFP	Productivity effect (*P*)	Innovation effect (*I*)	Correlations		
					GEI vs. TFP	GEI vs. *P*	GEI vs. *I*
Factor-driven economies	23.72	−0.34%	0.27%	−0.59%	0.13	0.47	−0.41
Efficiency-driven economies	39.21	1.69%	0.52%	1.17%	0.32	0.29	0.08
Innovation-driven economies	59.43	1.98%	0.42%	1.55%	0.24	0.05	0.33

the country) (innovation effect = −0.59%). In other words, although businesses in factor-driven economies are improving in the exploitation of the resources (productivity effect = 0.27%), this is not enough, and the failed attempts to introduce new technologies in these contexts—i.e., lacking appropriate social, cultural, economic, and structural conditions to capitalize on such innovations—explain the observed decline in total factor productivity.

Figure 4.2 plots the GEI score and the computed total factor productivity values. The correlation between TFP and GEI is 0.35 and the sign is positive (see Table 4.1). From the Fig. 4.2, we verify that the quality of the entrepreneurial ecosystem (GEI scores) and TFP moves in the same direction. Countries with a low-quality entrepreneurial ecosystem tend to show negative TFP values below unity. On contrary, all developed economies with supportive entrepreneurial ecosystems improve their total factor productivity, either by productivity or innovation effects (Table 4.2).

Figures 4.3 and 4.4 plot the relationship between the GEI index and the productivity and innovation effects, respectively. There is a positive association between entrepreneurship and the productivity effect (correlation = 0.09); however, this relationship is less pronounced than that found for the TFP. This result may well be partly explained by the differentiating impact of entrepreneurship over the productivity effect across economies. We observe that the correlation between entrepreneurship and the productivity effect scores the highest among factor-driven countries (0.47 in Table 4.3). Also, from Fig. 4.3 we note that in many underdeveloped and developing territories with low- and mid-level entrepreneurial ecosystem, the productivity effect is positive, while the result of the productivity effect for some developed economies is negative.

Thus, our results suggest that, in developing economies, the entrepreneurial ecosystem plays a much more decisive role on TFP via productivity improvements, that is, helping new and established businesses in developing economies to better exploit their limited resources, that is, "to do things better."

The picture is quite different when we look at the results for the innovation effect. The data in Table 4.3 show how the correlation between entrepreneurship and the innovation effect progressively increases as we move from factor-driven

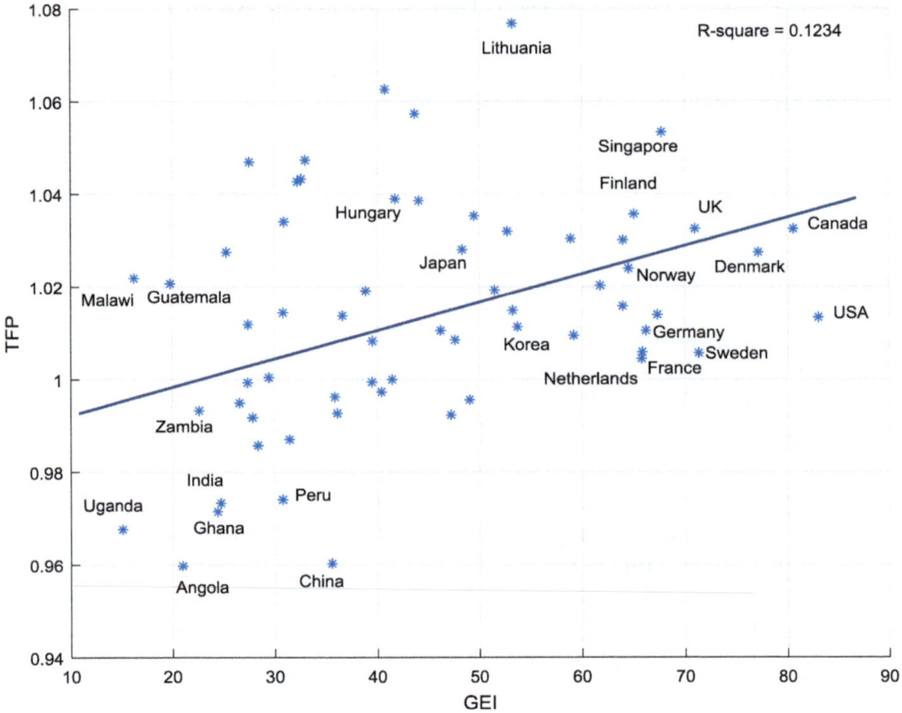

Fig. 4.2 GEI and total factor productivity

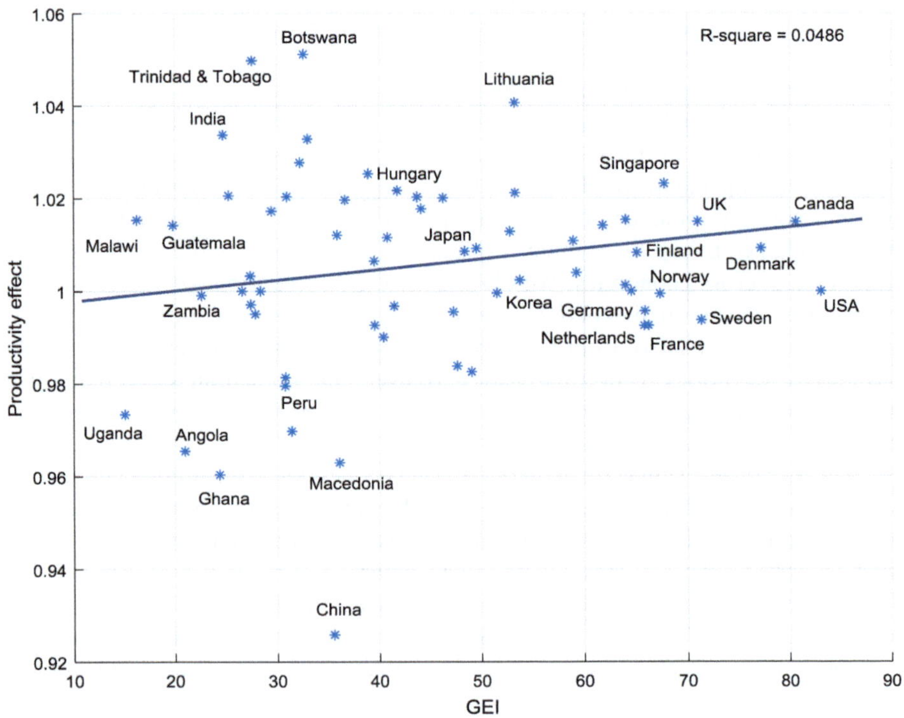

Fig. 4.3 GEI and the productivity effect

(correlation = −0.41) to innovation-driven economies (correlation = 0.33). Similarly, the impact of the innovation effect is much more potent in innovation-driven economies (1.55%) than in efficiency-driven (1.17%) and in factor-driven economies (−0.59%).

This trend is corroborated by the results in Fig. 4.4 in which we observe a steeper relationship between the GEI scores and the innovation effect. In contrast to the stronger effect of the entrepreneurial ecosystem over productivity in developing countries, we found that the positive influence of a healthy entrepreneurial ecosystem over the innovative capacity of new and established businesses is much more powerful in developed economies. With the exception of Turkey, the innovation effect linked to the efficient commercialization of innovations and new technologies is positive in all economies with high-quality entrepreneurial ecosystems (GEI > 50).

Based on the relationships reported above, the improvement of the entrepreneurial ecosystem (GEI scores) may well yield to improvements in total factor productivity via the enhanced capacity of businesses to use their available resources (productivity effect) and to exploit the market potential of new technologies and innovations. As a result, if every of the 64 analyzed countries raised its GEI score by 10%, the global total factor productivity will increase 0.22 TFP points, which represents an estimated improvement of 15.80%.[1] The country-by-country breakdown of the TFP improvement is presented in Table 4.4.

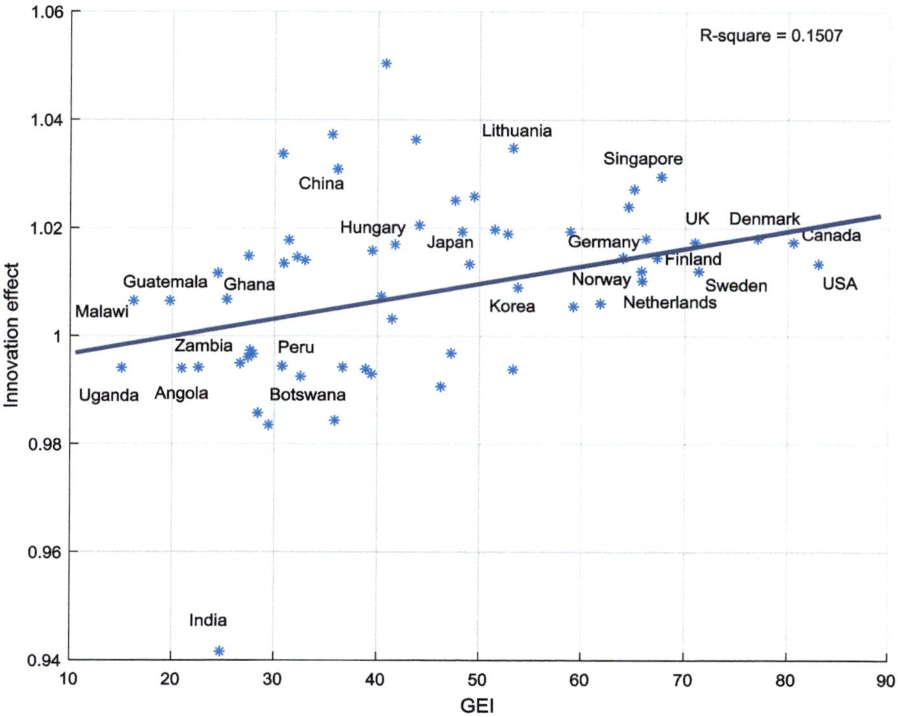

Fig. 4.4 GEI and the innovation effect

Table 4.4 Predicted increase in total factor productivity following a 10% improvement in GEI (values expressed in index points)

Country	Additional TFP	Additional productivity effect	Additional innovation effect	Country	Additional TFP	Additional productivity effect	Additional innovation effect
Algeria	0.15	0.06	0.12	Latvia	0.26	0.11	0.21
Angola	0.10	0.04	0.08	Lithuania	0.27	0.11	0.21
Argentina	0.18	0.07	0.14	Macedonia	0.18	0.07	0.14
Barbados	0.18	0.07	0.15	Malawi	0.08	0.03	0.07
Belgium	0.32	0.13	0.26	Malaysia	0.19	0.08	0.16
Bosnia and Herzegovina	0.14	0.06	0.11	Mexico	0.15	0.06	0.12
Botswana	0.16	0.07	0.13	Namibia	0.16	0.06	0.13
Brazil	0.13	0.05	0.10	Netherlands	0.33	0.13	0.26
Canada	0.40	0.16	0.32	Nigeria	0.14	0.06	0.11
Chile	0.31	0.12	0.25	Norway	0.32	0.13	0.26
China	0.18	0.07	0.14	Panama	0.16	0.06	0.13
Colombia	0.24	0.09	0.19	Peru	0.15	0.06	0.12
Croatia	0.20	0.08	0.16	Poland	0.23	0.09	0.18
Czech Republic	0.24	0.10	0.19	Portugal	0.25	0.10	0.20
Denmark	0.39	0.15	0.31	Romania	0.22	0.09	0.17
Ecuador	0.14	0.05	0.11	Russia	0.15	0.06	0.12
Estonia	0.29	0.12	0.24	Singapore	0.34	0.14	0.27
Finland	0.33	0.13	0.26	Slovakia	0.22	0.09	0.18

France	0.33	0.13	0.26	Slovenia	0.26	0.10	0.21
Germany	0.33	0.13	0.26	South Africa	0.20	0.08	0.16
Ghana	0.12	0.05	0.10	Spain	0.25	0.10	0.20
Greece	0.21	0.08	0.17	Sweden	0.36	0.14	0.29
Guatemala	0.10	0.04	0.08	Switzerland	0.34	0.13	0.27
Hungary	0.21	0.08	0.17	Thailand	0.16	0.07	0.13
India	0.12	0.05	0.10	Trinidad & Tobago	0.14	0.06	0.11
Iran	0.13	0.05	0.11	Turkey	0.27	0.11	0.21
Ireland	0.32	0.13	0.26	Uganda	0.08	0.03	0.06
Israel	0.30	0.12	0.24	United Kingdom	0.35	0.14	0.28
Italy	0.20	0.08	0.16	United States	0.42	0.17	0.33
Jamaica	0.14	0.05	0.11	Uruguay	0.20	0.08	0.16
Japan	0.24	0.10	0.19	Zambia	0.11	0.05	0.09
Korea	0.27	0.11	0.21				
Global Average	**0.22**	**0.09**	**0.18**				

Chapter 5
What Can We Do to Improve the Entrepreneurial Ecosystem?

A data-driven approach to improving entrepreneurial ecosystems begins with taking stock of the current state of the ecosystem through the lens of cross-country comparable data. However, the job does not end there. Once the strengths and weaknesses of an ecosystem have been identified, it is helpful to examine their underlying causes (see our original research on the South African entrepreneurial ecosystem). When these causes are understood, potential actions to improve the weakest pillars of a country's performance can be surfaced and evaluated. The selected actions depend not just on the characteristics of the ecosystem itself but also on the leverage points of the actor within the ecosystem. For example, it would not make sense for an incubator to solve a weakness in technology transfer by enacting national policy on STEM education—incubators don't have these levers available to them. Rather, each actor has a set of possible actions determined by their relationships to other components of the ecosystem: who they can influence and with what tools. By determining weaknesses, understanding the root causes of those weaknesses, and selecting actions appropriate to both the ecosystem *and the actor*, the odds of producing real change in an entrepreneurial ecosystem increase.

The following exercise demonstrates how the process discussed above might be carried out in an example ecosystem—South Africa.

South Africa's GEI data (visualized in the graphic below) shows that the country performs slightly better on the variables representing the traits of individuals than on those of institutions but that these two sets of variables are relatively balanced. Its scores on the 14 pillars of entrepreneurship vary between 7 out of 100 and 69 out of 100. This reveals that the most severe bottleneck in the South African entrepreneurial ecosystem is startup skills—measured by the perception that individual entrepreneurs have of their ability to start a business, combined with postsecondary education rates. These two variables capture startup skills from both the perspective of the entrepreneur and vis-à-vis the global economy.

Z. J. Ács et al., *Global Entrepreneurship and Development Index 2018*, SpringerBriefs in Economics, https://doi.org/10.1007/978-3-030-03279-1_5

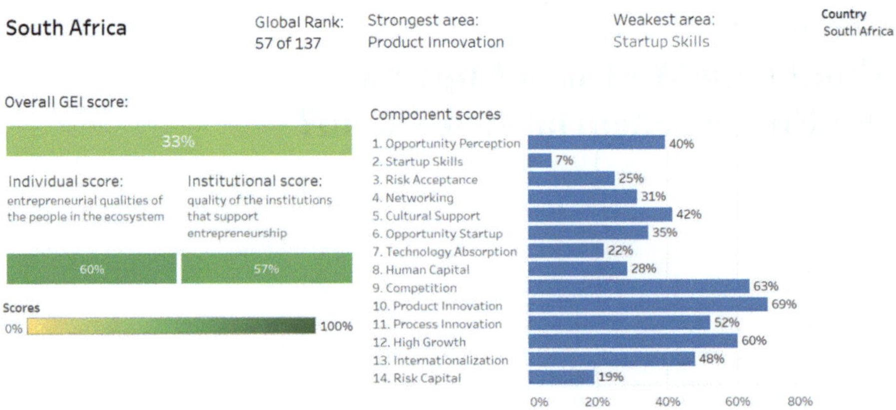

In GEDI's 2017 analysis of the entrepreneurial ecosystem of South Africa, we identified and mapped the causes and impacts of several ecosystem weaknesses by surveying entrepreneurs, investors, policymakers, and academics within the ecosystem. With respect to the startup skills bottleneck:

> *There are two facets to the skills and education bottlenecks as discussed by respondents: a lack of business skills among entrepreneurs and a lack of innovation curriculum in schools. The lack of business skills is connected with a lack of networks through which entrepreneurs discover their own knowledge gaps. Within the realm of basic (not entrepreneurship-specific) education, many respondents pointed out a lack of innovation curriculum and a system that favors employment over entrepreneurship.*
>
> *The cost of education was also listed as a cause of the follow-on lack in knowledge and skills and is particularly acute when combined with structural inequality and the failure of government programs to effectively address it.*
>
> *The factors listed by multiple respondents include the following: innovation not taught in schools (6), cost of education (5), education system which favors employment over entrepreneurship (4), quality of basic education (3), networks (2), and structural inequality (2).*

The position of South Africa within the global range of data, when coupled with the above additional insights on the causes and impacts of ecosystem bottlenecks, allows for a more nuanced selection of policy actions to address the startup skills gap in South Africa. Continuing the exercise begun above, we can now evaluate potential policy actions for a given ecosystem actor and bottleneck issue using the GEI actions matrix.

The GEI Actions Matrix

The Global Entrepreneurship and Development Index covers 14 areas (what we call pillars) of the entrepreneurship ecosystem. Each country has one or several critical areas that are holding back the ecosystem, and different actions can be taken to generate improvements in each of these areas. With the help of three experts—Professor Richard Saouma, Venture Capitalist Ken Krull, and Researcher Ainsley Lloyd—we've generated the following (non-exhaustive) list of example actions that one might take to impact each of the 14 areas measured by the GEI. We don't endorse all of these actions for all contexts but instead hope that this list helps start the conversation around improving the bottleneck issues in entrepreneurship ecosystems.

For the purposes of this exercise, let's assume the actor in question is a policymaker. Since we are taking the perspective of a policymaker, we'd look to the fifth column for actions that apply to our role. Since South Africa's most significant bottleneck is in startup skills, potential actions listed in that row of the matrix would be most relevant to improving the South African ecosystem of all of those listed in the matrix.

The relevant recommendations to consider in this case include the following:

- Expand access to tertiary education to a broader portion of the population.
- Offer tax credits for educational expenses.
- Implement tax-exempt educational savings plans.
- Create a policy to reduce the child workforce.
- Make high school business education mandatory, including the identification and capture of value.
- Fund regional initiatives to encourage student entrepreneurship, and make sure to prioritize underfunded initiatives.
- Offer funding with no strings attached to the student entrepreneur who gets the most traction on the least amount of resources.

Each of these actions represents a potential solution for a policymaker in addressing the startup skills bottleneck in South Africa.

As mentioned previously, the matrix is not exhaustive, and all listed actions are not necessarily appropriate for all country contexts. To illustrate how we might take this analysis further, consider the following recommendations for addressing the startup skills bottleneck. We produced these recommendations for our detailed report on the South African ecosystem, and they take into account additional factors unique to the South African ecosystem, such as structural inequality and a large informal sector.

Education: *A country that has the demographic structure of South Africa should make education the number one priority for all of South Africans. This is not a quick fix, but it is the only policy that cannot be ignored.*

Starting a business: *South Africa should be the easiest country in Africa to start a business on account of its well-developed infrastructure—not the hardest. South Africa ranks 131st on the ease of starting a business index. It ranks 111th in getting electricity services connected. South Africa should engage in a massive deregulation of the startup ecosystem process for all sectors of the population.*[1]

Employment training*: This is an ecosystem-centric unemployment/re-employment training program that prioritizes training of individuals without current employment options into new or existing firms or industries. For example, the United States offers an online service that matches the unemployed with training for jobs with new or existing firms.*[2]

[1] http://www.doingbusiness.org/rankings.

[2] http://www.unemployment-assist.com/index_adwords.html.

Area of the entrepreneurship ecosystem	What does it measure?	What can I do if I'm a(n)…		
		Entrepreneur	Large company	Policymaker
Opportunity perception	Can the population identify opportunities to start a business and does the institutional environment make it possible to act on those opportunities?	Expose yourself to new experiences to boost creative thinking Start a "side hustle" to test a business concept	Market and promote partnerships with entrepreneurial firms Create an entrepreneurship culture Create a policy of paid side project time (like Google) Bring attention to the entrepreneurial qualities of employees and how the firm empowers them to create value Show how the firm has partnered with entrepreneurs to help them launch businesses	Lower tax rates Promote entrepreneurial successes within economic development initiatives Advertise the success of local entrepreneurs who played by the book

Startup skills	Does the population have the skills necessary to start a business based on their own perceptions and the availability of tertiary education?	Ask entrepreneurs around you how they have developed the skills that have helped them be successful Participate in continuing education Learn a new skill Take an online course	Reimburse or match for continuing education Incorporate educational childcare and after-school care programs for working parents Sponsor skill building with local associations Emphasize the importance of entrepreneurship skills in collegiate recruitment programs at the pre-internship stage	Expand access to tertiary education to a broader portion of the population Offer tax credits for educational expenses Implement tax-exempt educational savings plans Create a policy to reduce the child workforce Make high school business education mandatory, including the identification and capture of value Fund regional initiatives to encourage student entrepreneurship, and make sure to prioritize underfunded initiatives Offer funding with no strings attached to the student entrepreneur who gets the most traction on the least amount of resources
Risk acceptance	Are individuals willing to take the risk of starting a business? Is the environment relatively low risk or do unstable institutions add additional risk to starting a business?	Run the smallest possible test you can run to validate your idea Predefine successful outcomes Recruit critical advisors willing to kill concepts that don't fit Realize that not all ideas can be implemented today or have a valid skill set match for the entrepreneur Identify external dependencies on your idea's success	Create an ok to fail culture Reward appropriate risk-taking behavior Help employees plan their efforts and log outcomes. The documentation process will help them realize that they take risk every day, and while they remember the failures, there are myriad daily wins	Improve institutional and regulatory stability and ensure absence of conflict Create simple and consistent personal and corporate bankruptcy processes Change the communication around social safety nets to highlight the fact that they are a great resource for potential entrepreneurs because they mitigate damages for those who fail

(continued)

Area of the entrepreneurship ecosystem	What does it measure?	What can I do if I'm a(n)…		
		Entrepreneur	Large company	Policymaker
Networking	Do entrepreneurs know each other and how geographically concentrated are their networks?	Find places where other entrepreneurs gather and engage (e.g., Kauffman Foundation's One Million Cups) Join a forum, club, association, or other group related to your concept	Sponsor formal networking functions as corporate recruiting Encourage mentorship Build formal intern and apprenticeship programs Host social events with entrepreneurs where they can learn what are the real pain points faced by companies, how they can add value, and/or what fish are too small for the large firm to fry	Improve ICT access and infrastructure Promote vertical associations' networking activities Sponsor an entrepreneurship week every 2 months. Showcase the work of startups in your area and invite the public Create "incubation space" in desolate areas in need of rejuvenation: empty cargo containers, a room with 4 walls that is available to would-be entrepreneurs, open 24/7
Cultural support	How does the country view entrepreneurship? Is it easy to choose entrepreneurship or does corruption make entrepreneurship difficult relative to other career paths?	Encourage and support entrepreneurs around you Create a blog or other appropriate social media around the developing of your entrepreneurial concept	Market entrepreneurship as formal company PR Sponsor recognition programs promoting entrepreneurship, like Entrepreneur of the Year programs Ensure that HR highlights the importance of entrepreneurial spirit to the entire pipeline of potential future employees, starting in high schools	Reduce and prevent corruption Track formal statistics on entrepreneurship and its effect on GPS and other institutional metrics Make it easy for firms to plug into communities to announce their values (entrepreneurship) in, e.g., high schools, by structuring formal slots or entrepreneurship days with the school system
Opportunity startup	Are entrepreneurs motivated by opportunity rather than necessity and does governance make the choice to be an entrepreneur easy?	Mentor or contribute to best practices in interacting with government and administrative overhead	Allow spinouts of corporate developed ideas that the company can't pursue	Reduce the administrative burden of paying taxes, and improve the capacity of the government to create and implement sound policies Lower the administrative overhead of incorporating and managing a business

Technology absorption	Is the technology sector large and can businesses rapidly absorb new technology?	Keep abreast of current technology and trends Invest in technology that furthers your business	Educate employees in current technology and trends Invest in technology partnerships that businesses align Sponsor after-school programming or similar STEM resources	Sponsor leading technologist at ecosystem events Promote local technologies and technologists Provide tax breaks for preferred industries. Sponsor STEM school programs
Human capital	Are entrepreneurs highly educated, well trained in business, and able to move freely in the labor market?	Invest in formal and informal continuing education	Reimburse or match for continuing education Incorporate educational childcare and after-school care programs for working parents Sponsor skill building with local associations	Foster a flexible labor market in which businesses can easily hire employees Sponsor students who leave home to pursue a better education, and tie the debt forgiveness to them returning, just like firms do with pre-MBA hires Sponsor free access to online learning platforms Provide tax breaks for education costs incurred by firms
Competition	Are entrepreneurs creating unique products and services and able to enter the market with them?	Identify opportunities within your market that are underserved or unique		Break up monopolies and policy anticompetitive practices
Product innovation	Is the country able to develop new products and integrate new technology?	Create products and services that are new to the market	Invest in R&D	Foster collaboration in research between universities and industry and the protection of intellectual property
Process innovation	Do businesses use new technology and are they able to access high-quality human capital in STEM fields?	Adopt new technology that improves your business's functioning		Improve the quality of scientific institutions and the availability of scientists and engineers

(continued)

Area of the entrepreneurship ecosystem	What does it measure?	What can I do if I'm a(n)…		
		Entrepreneur	Large company	Policymaker
High growth	Do businesses intend to grow and have the strategic capacity to achieve this growth?	Set ambitious goals for hiring and profits		Reduce the barriers to obtaining equity financing
Internationalization	Do entrepreneurs want to enter global markets and is the economy complex enough to produce ideas that are valuable globally?	Identify opportunities to export your products/ services to new markets		Facilitate the interaction of individuals in increasingly complex networks in order to make products
Risk capital	Is capital available from both individual and institutional investors?	Support other entrepreneurs with seed funding	Support entrepreneurs in corporate philanthropy, impact and social responsibility initiatives	Reduce the barriers to providing venture capital and private equity financing

Informal to formal: *Legitimize a pathway to formal entrepreneurship in the informal sector. It is important for enterprises to be able to become a part of the formal economy in order to grow the businesses and ensure that firms pay taxes. However, entering the formal economy should not and cannot be a burden on SMEs.*[3] *"Some people are self-employed in the informal sector because they want to avoid registration and taxation. But many people work in the informal sector through necessity, not choice. Today, there are two features of the informal sector that are well-recognized. Firstly, much of the informal economy contributes greatly to the formal economy. Secondly, women constitute the majority of precarious, under-paid, informal workers."*[4]

Wage subsidies can be used to address structural inequality: *A randomized control trial (RCT) of a wage subsidy voucher "led to a higher employment one year after receiving the voucher. This impact is relatively large – between 5.4 and 7.4 percentage points. Given that only 24 percent of those not in wage employment in the control group in 2010 transitioned into employment in 2011 and overall only 31 percent of those in the control group were in wage employment in 2011 these results suggest that the voucher increased employment by 24 percent."*[5] *Such an intervention addresses "a troubling equilibrium... [where]... the demand for labor is lower than it would be if workers' types were observable (since firms hire based on expected skill levels), the incentives to obtain skills are diminished (since workers cannot be sure they will reap the benefits of their acquired skills). Wage subsidies provided to SMEs could be particularly impactful in terms of both unemployment and the affordability of skilled labor."*

The above process illustrates how one might arrive at a list of actions to improve an ecosystem, beginning first with the global data, incorporating causal analysis, considering unique ecosystem characteristics, and selecting for actions that are available to a given type of actor in the ecosystem.

[3] http://www.ilo.org/wcmsp5/groups/public/%2D%2D-ed_norm/%2D%2D-relconf/documents/meetingdocument/wcms_218128.pdf.

[4] http://blogs.worldbank.org/jobs/moving-informal-formal-sector-and-what-it-means-policymakers.

[5] Levinsohn, J., Rankin, N., Roberts, G., & Schöer, V. (2014). Wage subsidies and youth employment in South Africa: Evidence from a randomized control trial. Stellenbosch economic working papers 02/14.

Chapter 6
Methodology and Data Description

Introduction

In previous GEI publications, we have described the Global Entrepreneurship and Development Index methodology in detail.[1] Here we describe the structure of the dataset and a short summary of the GEI methodology. As compared to the previous versions, the institutional components of the GEI have been reviewed and changed. Here, we provide a description of the changes. As a result, the previous scores and rankings cannot be compared to this version.

The Structure of the Index

We have defined country-level entrepreneurship as "the dynamic, institutionally embedded interaction between entrepreneurial attitudes, entrepreneurial abilities, and entrepreneurial aspirations by individuals, which drives the allocation of resources through the creation and operation of new ventures."[2] According to this definition, we propose four-level index building: (1) variables, (2) pillars, (3) sub-indices, and, finally, (4) the super-index. All three sub-indices contain several pillars, which can be interpreted as the quasi-independent building blocks of this entrepreneurship index.

In this section, we describe the sub-indices and pillars. In the following section, we describe the variables. The three sub-indices of attitudes, abilities, and aspirations constitute the entrepreneurship super-index, which we call the Global

[1] See Acs and Szerb (2009, 2012), Acs, Szerb, and Autio (2013, 2014, 2016).

[2] See Acs, Szerb, and Autio (2014) p. 480.

Z. J. Ács et al., *Global Entrepreneurship and Development Index 2018*,
SpringerBriefs in Economics, https://doi.org/10.1007/978-3-030-03279-1_6

Entrepreneurship and Development Index. While in Chap. 2 we have provided a detailed portrayal of the GEI components, here we focus on the measurement of the particular variables and pillars. The structure of the index is in Table 6.1.

Table 6.1 The structure of the new Global Entrepreneurship and Development Index (GEI)[a]

Global Entrepreneurship and Development Index	Sub-indexes	Pillars	Variables (ind./inst.)
	Attitude sub-index	Opportunity perception	*Opportunity recognition*
			Freedom (economic freedom*property rights)
		Startup skills	*Skill perception*
			Education (tertiary education*quality of education)
		Risk acceptance	*Risk perception*
			Country risk
		Networking	*Know entrepreneurs*
			Agglomeration (urbanization*infrastructure)
		Cultural support	*Career status*
			Corruption
	Ability sub-index	Opportunity startup	*Opportunity motivation*
			Governance (taxation*good governance)
		Technology absorption	*Technology level*
			Technology absorption
		Human capital	*Educational level*
			Labor market (staff training*labor freedom)
		Competition	*Competitors*
			Competitiveness (market dominance*regulation)
	Aspiration sub-index	Product innovation	*New product*
			Tech transfer
		Process innovation	*New technology*
			Science (GERD*((average quality of scientifical institutions +availability of scientists and engineers))
		High growth	*Gazelle*
			Finance and strategy (venture capital*business sophistication)
		Internationalization	*Export*
			Economic complexity
		Risk capital	*Informal investment*
			Depth of capital market

[a]Individual variables are colored with white background while institutional ones with light blue background

Entrepreneurial attitudes reflect the people's attitudes toward entrepreneurship. It involves opportunity recognition, startup skills, risk perception, networking, and cultural supports of entrepreneurs. Institutional embedding is expressed as the property rights and economic freedom, the quality of the education, the riskiness of the country, the connectivity potential, and the prevalence of corruption.

Entrepreneurial abilities include some important characteristics of the entrepreneur that determine the extent to which new startups will have potential for growth, such as motivation based on opportunity as opposed to necessity, the potential technology intensity of the startup, the entrepreneur's level of education, the level of competition, and digital startup capabilities. These individual factors coincide with the proper institutional factors of taxation and the efficiency of government operation (governance), technology adsorption capability, the freedom of the labor market and the extent of staff training (labor market), and the dominance of powerful business groups as well as the effectiveness of anti-monopoly regulation (regulation).

Entrepreneurial aspiration refers to the distinctive, qualitative, strategy-related nature of entrepreneurial activity. The individual and institutional factors of product and process innovation such as technology transfer, the applied research potential of science, high growth expectations, venture capital availability and strategy sophistication (finance and strategy), internationalization, and the availability of risk financing constitute entrepreneurial aspirations. Table 6.2 provides a short description and interpretation of the pillars we apply.

By applying the Penalty for Bottleneck approach, the GEI methodology captures the notion that systems, by definition, comprise multiple components and that these components co-produce system performance. These are defining characteristics of any system, which simple summative indices fail to capture. In a simple summative index, each system component contributes directly and independently to system performance. In the context of entrepreneurship, this would mean, for example, that a national measure of education would, directly and independent of other system components, contribute to "national entrepreneurship," while in reality we know that education cannot contribute much to a country's entrepreneurial performance if individuals fail to act. On the other hand, if education were absent, the economic potential of entrepreneurial entries would be severely constrained. Moreover, even if both education and agency were present, country-level entrepreneurial performance would be constrained if, for example, growth aspirations were missing or if there were no financial resources available to feed the growth of new ventures. A simple summative index would fail to recognize such interactions, thereby ignoring crucial aspects of system-level performance.

The Individual Variables and Dataset

As mentioned previously, an entrepreneurship index should incorporate both individual-level and institutional/environmental variables. All individual-level variables are from the GEM survey. The institutional variables are obtained from

Table 6.2 The description of the GEI pillars

Pillar name	Description
Opportunity perception	Opportunity perception refers to the entrepreneurial opportunity perception potential of the population and weights this against the freedom of the country and property rights
Startup skills	Startup skill captures the perception of startup skills in the population and weights this aspect with the quality of education
Risk acceptance	Risk acceptance captures the inhibiting effect of fear of failure of the population on entrepreneurial action combined with a measure of the country's risk
Networking	This pillar combines two aspects of networking: (1) a proxy of the ability of potential and active entrepreneurs to access and mobilize opportunities and resources and (2) the ease of access to reach each other
Cultural support	The cultural support pillar combines how positively a given country's inhabitants view entrepreneurs in terms of status and career choice and how the level of corruption in that country affects this view
Opportunity startup	The opportunity startup pillar captures the prevalence of individuals who pursue potentially better-quality opportunity-driven startups (as opposed to necessity-driven startups) weighted with the combined effect of taxation and government quality of services
Technology absorption	The technology absorption pillar reflects the technology intensity of a country's startup activity combined with a country's capacity for firm-level technology absorption
Human capital	The human capital pillar captures the quality of entrepreneurs as weighing the percentage of startups founded by individuals with higher than secondary education with a qualitative measure of the propensity of firms in a given country to train their staff combined with the freedom of the labor market
Competition	The competition pillar measures the level of the product or market uniqueness of startups combined with the market power of existing businesses and business groups as well as with the effectiveness of competitive regulation
Product innovation	The product innovation pillar captures the tendency of entrepreneurial firms to create new products weighted by the technology transfer capacity of a country
Process innovation	The process innovation pillar captures the use of new technologies by startups combined with the gross domestic expenditure on research and development (GERD) and the potential of a country to conduct applied research
High growth	The high growth pillar is a combined measure of (1) the percentage of high-growth businesses that intend to employ at least 10 people and plan to grow more than 50 percent in 5 years (2) the availability of venture capital and (3) business strategy sophistication
Internationalization	The internationalization pillar captures the degree to which a country's entrepreneurs are internationalized, as measured by businesses' exporting potential weighted by the level of economic complexity of the country
Risk capital	The risk capital pillar combines two measures of finance: informal investment in startups and a measure of the depth of the capital market. Availability of risk capital is to fulfill growth aspirations

Source: Own creation

various sources. The full list and description of the applied GEM individual variables can be seen in Table 6.3.

For the 2018 GEI publication, we used 2015–2016 or previous years' Global Entrepreneurship Monitor individual data. For the individual variable calculation, we include 529,466 individuals from 102 countries of the GEM Adult Population Survey; 65 countries' individual data are from the years 2015–2016, and 37 countries have individual data from the pre-2014 years. We estimated the individual variables for 35 countries by using nearby and similar countries' GEM

Table 6.3 The description of the individual variables used in the GEI

Individual variable	Description
Opportunity recognition	The percentage of the 18–64 aged population recognizing good conditions to start business next 6 months in area he/she lives
Skill perception	The percentage of the 18–64 aged population claiming to possess the required knowledge/skills to start a business
Risk perception	The percentage of the 18–64 aged population stating that the fear of failure would not prevent starting a business
Know entrepreneurs	The percentage of the 18–64 aged population knowing someone who started a business in the past 2 years
Career	The percentage of the 18–64 aged population saying that people consider starting business as good career choice
Status	The percentage of the 18–64 aged population thinking that people attach high status to successful entrepreneurs
Career status	The status and respect of entrepreneurs calculated as the average of career and status
Opportunity motivation	Percentage of the TEA businesses initiated because of opportunity startup motive
Technology level	Percentage of the TEA businesses that are active in technology sectors (high or medium)
Educational level	Percentage of the TEA businesses owner/managers having participated over secondary education
Competitors	Percentage of the TEA businesses started in those markets where not many businesses offer the same product
New product	Percentage of the TEA businesses offering products that are new to at least some of the customers
New technology	Percentage of the TEA businesses using new technology that is less than 5 years old on average (including 1 year)
Gazelle	Percentage of the TEA businesses having high job expectation average (over 10 more employees and 50% in 5 years)
Export	Percentage of the TEA businesses where at least some customers are outside country (over 1%)
Informal Investment Mean	The mean amount of 3-year informal investment
Business angel	The percentage of the population aged 18–64 who provided funds for new business in the past 3 years, excluding stocks and funds, average
Informal investment	The amount of informal investment calculated as INFINVMEAN* BUSANG

Adult Population Survey data. It is important to note that any estimation involves a potential of higher error term as compared to those countries that participated in the regular GEM survey. Therefore, the pillar scores, the sub-indices, and the GEI scores based on estimated individual data should be viewed with discretion.

Since the availability of the institutional data also limited the selection of the countries, we could involve only those nations that participated in the World Economic Forum 2015–2016 or 2016–2017 Global Competitiveness Report (GCR) survey. Some GCR countries were left out because of the lack of similar or nearby GEM countries. The size of the sample in different years, the participating countries, and the calculation of the individual variables, including the 35 non-GEM countries, are also reported in Table 6.4. All analyses of countries having data older than 2014 and based on estimation should be handled with caution and cannot be used for any policy suggestions. This is particularly true for countries with estimated individual data.[3] In fact, even GEM survey-backed calculated variables and pillars are only the starting point of a detailed GEI-based policy analysis.[4]

The Institutional Variables and Dataset

Since the GEM lacks the necessary institutional variables, we complement individual variables with other widely used relevant data from Transparency International (Corruption Perceptions Index), UNESCO (tertiary education enrollment, GERD), World Economic Forum (infrastructure, regulation, scientific institutions, availability of scientists, business sophistication, technology absorption and technology transfer capability, staff training, market dominance, venture capital), United Nations (urbanization), The Heritage Foundation and World Bank (economic freedom, property rights, labor freedom), the World Bank (taxation, good governance), the Observatory of Economic Complexity (economic complexity), OECD (country

[3] Based on our experience, when a country eventually joins GEM, the actual data produced tends to be very similar to our estimates. We have collected those 11 countries that joined GEM over the 2012–2015 time period for which we previously estimated their data points. Out of the 11 countries, GEI scores were within the 10% range of differences including Botswana, Burkina Faso, Estonia, Malawi, Namibia, Qatar, and Senegal. Three countries—Cameroon, El Salvador, and Ethiopia—are within the 20% range, and the only large difference in calculation is Bulgaria. Bulgaria has proved to be a major outlier in the European Union, just as nearly every dataset has outliers. It seems that we did provide fair estimations for all the African countries. When you evaluate these estimation results, do not forget that all data collection has an error term since we use samples and not the full population. In fact the error term in Bulgaria, based on the Total Early-Phased Entrepreneurial Activity (TEA), appears to be very high. For more information on the application of estimated data, see our website https://thegedi.org/the-value-of-estimation-creating-reference-points-for-countries-with-missing-data/.

[4] For detailed policy analysis, see Autio and Levie (2015), Estonia report (2015).

Table 6.4 The distribution of the sample by countries and the calculation of the individual variables

Country/year	2009	2010	2011	2012	2013	2014	2015	2016	Individual variable method of calculation
Albania									Average of Bosnia 2014 and Macedonia 2016
Algeria				4984	2497				Average of 2012–2013
Angola					2049	2028			Average of 2013–2014
Argentina							2519	1679	Average of 2015–2016
Armenia									Average of Georgia and Russia
Australia							1770	1593	Average of 2015–2016
Austria						4554		4581	Average of 2014–2016
Azerbaijan									Average of Georgia and Turkey
Bahrain									Same as Qatar 2016
Bangladesh			1932						2011
Barbados						2000	2000		Average of 2014–2015
Belgium						2004	2022		Average of 2014–2015
Belize								2267	Average of 2014 and 2016
Benin						2000			2014
Bolivia						2590			2014
Bosnia and Herzegovina					2004	2015			Average of 2013–2014
Botswana						2146	2200		Average of 2014–2015
Brazil							2000	2000	Average of 2015–2016
Brunei Darussalam									Average of Malaysia 2016 and Singapore 2014
Bulgaria							2001	2000	Average of 2015–2016
Burkina Faso							2325	2325	Average of 2015–2016
Burundi									Average of Burkina Faso and Cameroon

(continued)

Table 6.4 (continued)

Country/year	2009	2010	2011	2012	2013	2014	2015	2016	Individual variable method of calculation
Cambodia									Average of Vietnam 2015 and Thailand
Cameroon							2397	2413	Average of 2015–2016
Canada							2933	1767	Average of 2015–2016
Chad									Average of Burkina Faso and Cameroon
Chile							5407	7961	Average of 2015–2016
China							3365	3513	Average of 2015–2016
Colombia							3686	2069	Average of 2015–2016
Costa Rica				2041		2057			Average of 2012–2014
Côte d'Ivoire									Average of Burkina Faso and Cameroon
Croatia						2000	2000		Average of 2015–2016
Cyprus								2000	Only 2016
Czech Republic					5009			2001	2013
Denmark				2217		2008			Average of 2012–2014
Dominican Republic	2007								2009
Ecuador							1931	1841	Average of 2015–2016
Egypt				2501			2512	2528	Average of 2015–2016
El Salvador						2014		1753	Average of 2014 and 2016
Estonia							2002	1993	Average of 2015–2016
Ethiopia				3003					2012
Finland							2007	2018	Average of 2015–2016
France					1567	1567		1541	Average of 2014 and 2016
Gabon									Average of Namibia 2014 and Botswana 2015

(continued)

Table 6.4 (continued)

Country/year	2009	2010	2011	2012	2013	2014	2015	2016	Individual variable method of calculation
The Gambia									Average of Burkina Faso and Cameroon
Georgia						1648		1579	Average of 2014 and 2016
Germany							3842	3944	Average of 2015–2016
Ghana				2213	2100				Average of 2012–2013
Greece							2000	2000	Average of 2015–2016
Guatemala							2181	2219	Average of 2015–2016
Guinea									Average of Burkina Faso and Cameroon
Guyana									Same as Suriname 2014
Honduras									Average of Guatemala and Panama
Hong Kong								1783	Only 2016
Hungary							2000	2011	Average of 2015–2016
Iceland		1684							2010
India							3413	3400	Average of 2015–2016
Indonesia							5620	3464	Average of 2015–2016
Iran							3234	3295	Average of 2015–2016
Ireland							2001	2004	Average of 2015–2016
Israel							2055	2516	Average of 2015–2016
Italy							2000	2045	Average of 2015–2016
Jamaica					2246	2637		2020	Average of 2014 and 2016
Japan					2000	2006			Average of 2013–2014
Jordan								1830	Only 2016
Kazakhstan							2101	2086	Average of 2015–2016

(continued)

Table 6.4 (continued)

Country/year	2009	2010	2011	2012	2013	2014	2015	2016	Individual variable method of calculation
Kenya									Average of Burkina Faso and Cameroon
Korea							2000	2000	Average of 2015–2016
Kuwait									Same as Qatar
Kyrgyz Republic									Average of Kazakhstan and Russia
Lao PDR									Average of Vietnam 2015 and Thailand
Latvia							2004	1625	Average of 2015–2016
Lebanon							2600	2600	Average of 2015–2016
Liberia									Average of Burkina Faso and Cameroon
Libya					2246				2013
Lithuania					2000	2000			Average of 2013–2014
Luxembourg							2016	2024	Average of 2015–2016
Macedonia							1998	1991	Average of 2015–2016
Madagascar									Average of Burkina Faso and Cameroon
Malawi				1847	2094				Average of 2012–2013
Malaysia							2000	2005	Average of 2015–2016
Mali									Average of Burkina Faso and Cameroon
Mauritania									Average of Burkina Faso and Cameroon
Mexico							4643	5111	Average of 2015–2016
Moldova									Average of Romania 2015 and Russia
Montenegro		2000							2010
Morocco							2061	2005	Average of 2015–2016
Mozambique									Average of Burkina Faso and Cameroon

(continued)

Table 6.4 (continued)

Country/year	2009	2010	2011	2012	2013	2014	2015	2016	Individual variable method of calculation
Myanmar									Average of Vietnam 2015 and Thailand
Namibia				1959	1938				Average of 2012–2013
Netherlands							1754	1768	Average of 2015–2016
Nicaragua									Average of Guatemala and Panama
Nigeria				2651	2604				Average of 2012–2013
Norway						2000	2000		Average of 2014–2015
Oman									Same as Qatar 2016
Pakistan			2002	2000					Average of 2011–2012
Panama							2000	2015	Average of 2015–2016
Paraguay									Average of Ecuador and Peru
Peru							2078	2080	Average of 2015–2016
Philippines						2000	2000		Average of 2014–2015
Poland							2000	1623	Average of 2015–2016
Portugal							2005	2003	Average of 2015–2016
Puerto Rico							1999	1998	Average of 2015–2016
Qatar						4269		2980	Average of 2014 and 2016
Romania						1998	2002		Average of 2014–2015
Russia						2001		2007	Average of 2014 and 2016
Rwanda									Average of Burkina Faso and Cameroon
Saudi Arabia								4049	Only 2016
Senegal							2363		2015
Serbia	1766								2009
Sierra Leone									Average of Burkina Faso and Cameroon

(continued)

Table 6.4 (continued)

Country/year	2009	2010	2011	2012	2013	2014	2015	2016	Individual variable method of calculation
Singapore					1998	2004			Average of 2013–2014
Slovakia							2003	2000	Average of 2015–2016
Slovenia							2009	1621	Average of 2015–2016
South Africa							2765	2862	Average of 2015–2016
Spain							24300	22000	Average of 2015–2016
Sri Lanka									Same as India
Suriname					2074	2006			Average of 2013–2014
Swaziland									Average of Namibia 2014 and Botswana 2015
Sweden							3716	3663	Average of 2015–2016
Switzerland							1886	2834	Average of 2015–2016
Taiwan							2000	2000	Average of 2015–2016
Tajikistan									Average of Kazakhstan and Russia
Tanzania									Average of Burkina Faso and Cameroon
Thailand							3000	2693	Average of 2015–2016
Trinidad and Tobago					1787	1769			Average of 2013–2014
Tunisia							1946		2015
Turkey					32945			2411	Average of 2013 and 2016
Uganda					2513	2112			Average of 2013–2014
Ukraine									Average of Romania 2015 and Russia
United Arab Emirates								2011	2016
United Kingdom							7886	8224	Average of 2015–2016
United States							2683	2573	Average of 2015–2016

(continued)

Table 6.4 (continued)

Country/year	2009	2010	2011	2012	2013	2014	2015	2016	Individual variable method of calculation
Uruguay							1742	1615	Average of 2015–2016
Venezuela			1888						2011
Vietnam						2000	2000		Average of 2014–2015
Zambia				2155	2099				Average of 2012–2013

risk), and the Venture Capital and Private Equity Country Attractiveness Index (depth of capital market[5]).

In this version, we apply the most recent institutional variables available on May 31, 2017. The full description of the institutional variables, their sources, and the year of the survey can be found in Table 6.5.

Missing Variables and Data Imputations

Since our basic individual data are provided by the GEM, participation in the GEM survey determines the potential list of countries and sample size. However, there is another potential limitation, the availability of institutional data. Because 7 out of our 14 institutional variables are from the GCI, it is particularly important to have these variables. While there were five additional countries in the GEM 2014 surveys, we had to cancel out Tonga, Vanuatu, the West Bank and Gaza Strip, Yemen, and Syria because of the lack of proper institutional variables.[6]

A few variables are missing for some countries. Since we did not want to drop any more countries from the sample, we estimated the missing data using expert techniques, as follows: the GERD measure lacked data for Angola, Bangladesh, Belize, Benin, Cameroon, Chad, Côte d'Ivoire, Guinea, Libya, Malawi, Mauritania, Namibia, Oman, Qatar, Rwanda, Sierra Leone, Suriname , Swaziland, Tanzania, and Venezuela. In these cases, other government sources and data from similar nearby countries provided adequate estimates. Economic complexity data for Armenia, Azerbaijan, Brunei Darussalam, Guinea, Kyrgyz Republic, Montenegro, Myanmar, Swaziland, and Tajikistan are estimated similarly to the GERD, by applying nearby country data points. Puerto Rico's business freedom dataset is the

[5] Groh, Liechtenstein, and Lieser (2012a, 2012b).

[6] Some may not consider the West Bank and Gaza Strip an independent country. Tonga and Vanuatu are tiny countries, and Yemen and Syria have been engaged in civil war over the last few years.

Table 6.5 The description and source of the institutional variables used in the GEI

Institutional variable	Description	Source of data	Data availability
Economic freedom	"Business freedom is a quantitative measure of the ability to start, operate, and close a business that represents the overall burden of regulation, as well as the efficiency of government in the regulatory process. The business freedom score for each country is a number between 0 and 100, with 100 equaling the freest business environment. The score is based on 10 factors, all weighted equally, using data from the World Bank's Doing Business study" (http://www.heritage.org/Index/pdf/Index09_Methodology.pdf). Data are collected from 2016	Heritage Foundation/ World Bank	http://www.heritage.org/index/explore.aspx
Property rights	"The property rights component is an assessment of the ability of individuals to accumulate private property, secured by clear laws that are fully enforced by the state. It measures the degree to which a country's laws protect private property rights and the degree to which its government enforces those laws. It also assesses the likelihood that private property will be expropriated and analyzes the independence of the judiciary, the existence of corruption within the judiciary, and the ability of individuals and businesses to enforce contracts" (http://www.heritage.org/index/property-rights)	Heritage Foundation/ World Bank	http://www.heritage.org/index/explore.aspx
Freedom and property	Economic freedom * property rights	Own calculation	
Tertiary education	Gross enrollment ratio in tertiary education, 2016 or latest available data	World Bank	http://data.worldbank.org/indicator/SE.TER.ENRR
Quality of education	Answers to the question: "In your country, how do you assess the quality of math and science education? [1 = extremely poor – among the worst in the world; 7 = excellent – among the best in the world]"		The Global Competitiveness Report 2016–2017, p. 375

(continued)

Table 6.5 (continued)

Institutional variable	Description	Source of data	Data availability
Education	Tertiary education * quality of education	Own calculation	
Country risk	The country risk classifications are meant to reflect country risk. Under the participants' system, country risk is composed of transfer and convertibility risk (i.e., the risk a government imposes capital or exchange controls that prevent an entity from converting local currency into foreign currency and/or transferring funds to creditors located outside the country) and cases of force majeure (e.g. war, expropriation, revolution, civil disturbance, floods, earthquakes). 2017	OECD	http://www.oecd.org/trade/xcred/cre-crc-historical-internet-english.pdf
Urbanization	Urbanization that is the percentage of the population living in urban areas; data are from the Population Division of the United Nations, 2016 or latest available data	United Nations	http://data.worldbank.org/indicator/SP.URB.TOTL.IN.ZS
Infrastructure	Pillar 2, infrastructure in the World Competitiveness Report: "Extensive and efficient infrastructure is critical for ensuring the effective functioning of the economy"	World Economic Forum	The Global Competitiveness Report 2016–2017, p. 35
Connectivity	Urbanization * infrastructure	Own calculation	
Corruption	The Corruption Perceptions Index (CPI) measures the perceived level of public sector corruption in a country. "The CPI is a 'survey of surveys,' based on 13 different expert and business surveys" (http://www.transparency.org/policy_research/surveys_indices/cpi/2009). Overall performance is measured on a 10-point Likert scale. Data are collected over the last 24 months	Transparency International	https://www.transparency.org/news/feature/corruption_perceptions_index_2016#table

(continued)

Table 6.5 (continued)

Institutional variable	Description	Source of data	Data availability
Taxation	Paying taxes scores "(…) addresses the taxes and mandatory contributions that a medium-size company must pay or withhold in a given year, as well as measures the administrative burden in paying taxes" (http://www.doingbusiness.org/data/exploretopics/paying-taxes)	World Bank	http://www.doingbusiness.org/data/distance-to-frontier
Good governance	The effectiveness of the government and "the capacity of the government to effectively formulate and implement sound policies" (http://info.worldbank.org/governance/wgi/#home)	World Bank	http://qog.pol.gu.se/data/datadownloads/qogbasicdata
Taxgovern	Measures the effectiveness of using the taxes by combining together the level of the tax by the quality of government services, taxation* good governance	Own calculation	
Tech absorption	Firm-level technology absorption capability: "In your country, to what extent do businesses adopt the latest technologies? [1 = not at all; 7 = to a great extent])"	World Economic Forum	The Global Competitiveness Report 2016–2017. p. 377
Labor freedom	Measures the freedom of the labor as "(...) that considers various aspects of the legal and regulatory framework of a country's labor market, including regulations concerning minimum wages, laws inhibiting layoffs, severance requirements, and measurable regulatory restraints on hiring and hours worked" (http://www.heritage.org/index/labor-freedom)	Heritage Foundation	http://www.heritage.org/index/download
Staff training	The extent of staff training: "To what extent do companies in your country invest in training and employee development? (1 = hardly at all; 7 = to a great extent)"	World Economic Forum	The Global Competitiveness Report 2016–2017, p. 391
Labor market	Labor freedom * staff training		
Regulation	Effectiveness of anti-monopoly policy, answering to the question: "In your country, how effective are anti-monopoly policies at ensuring fair competition? [1 = not effective at all; 7 = extremely effective]"	World Economic Forum	The Global Competitiveness Report 2016–2017, p. 391

(continued)

Table 6.5 (continued)

Institutional variable	Description	Source of data	Data availability
Market dominance	Extent of market dominance: "In your country, how do you characterize corporate activity? [1 = dominated by a few business groups; 7 = spread among many firms]"	World Economic Forum	The Global Competitiveness Report 2016–2017, p. 375
Compregulation	Regulation * market dominance		
Technology Transfer	These are the innovation index points from GCI: a complex measure of innovation Including investment in research and development (R&D) by the private sector, the presence of high-quality scientific research institutions and the collaboration in research between universities and industry, and the protection of intellectual property	World Economic Forum	The Global Competitiveness Report 2016–2017, p. 44-45
GERD	Gross domestic expenditure on research and development (GERD) as a percentage of GDP; year 2014 or latest available data in Puerto Rico, Dominican Republic, and the United Arab Emirates are estimated	UNESCO	http://data.uis.unesco.org/?ReportId=2656
Scientific institutions	Quality of scientific research institutions. Answering to the question: "In your country, how do you assess the quality of scientific research institutions? [1 = extremely poor – among the worst in the world; 7 = extremely good – among the best in the world]"	World Economic Forum	The Global Competitiveness Report 2016–2017, p. 379
Availability of scientist	Availability of scientists and engineers. Answering to the question: "In your country, to what extent are scientists and engineers available? [1 = not at all; 7 = widely available]"	World Economic Forum	The Global Competitiveness Report 2016–2017, p. 379
Science	GERD* average of scientific institutions and availability of scientist	Own calculation	

(continued)

Table 6.5 (continued)

Institutional variable	Description	Source of data	Data availability
Venture capital	Venture capital availability. Answering to the question: "In your country, how easy is it for startup entrepreneurs with innovative but risky projects to obtain equity funding? [1 = extremely difficult; 7 = extremely easy]"	World Economic Forum	The Global Competitiveness Report 2016–2017, p. 377
Business strategy	Refers to the ability of companies to pursue distinctive strategies, which involves differentiated positioning and innovative means of production and service delivery	World Economic Forum	The Global Competitiveness Report 2016–2017, p. 44-45
Finance and strategy	Venture capital business strategy	Own calculation	
Economic complexity	"The complexity of an economy is related to the multiplicity of useful knowledge embedded in it. Because individuals are limited in what they know, the only way societies can expand their knowledge base is by facilitating the interaction of individuals in increasingly complex networks in order to make products. We can measure economic complexity by the mix of these products that countries are able to make" (http://atlas.media.mit.edu/en/resources/economic_complexity/)	Observatory of Economic Complexity	http://atlas.media.mit.edu/en/rankings/country/eci/
Depth of capital market[a]	The depth of capital market is one of the six sub-indices of the Venture Capital and Private Equity index. This variable is a complex measure of the size and liquidity of the stock market, level of IPO, M&A, and debt and credit market activity. Note that there were some methodological changes over the 2006–2015 time period, so previous years' comparison is not perfect	EMLYON Business School, France, and IESE Business School, Barcelona, Spain	http://blog.iese.edu/vcpeindex/

[a]Special thanks to Alexander Groh and his team for providing the depth of capital market data

same as the United States. All the other data are available for all countries; therefore, we believe that these rough estimates do not influence our results noticeably.[7]

Calculating the Scores

The GEI scores for all the countries are calculated according to the following eight points.

1. *The selection of variables:* We start with the variables that come directly from the original sources for each country involved in the analysis. The variables can be at the individual level (personal or business) that are coming from the GEM Adult Population Survey or the institutional/environmental level that are coming from various other sources. Altogether we use 16 individual and 15 institutional variables.
2. *The construction of the pillars:* We calculate all pillars from the variables using the interaction variable method, that is, by multiplying the individual variable with the proper institutional variable.

$$z_{i,j} = \mathrm{IND}_{i,j} * \mathrm{INS}_{i,j} \tag{6.1}$$

for all $j = 1, \ldots, k$, the number of individual, institutional variables, and pillars.

$\mathrm{IND}_{i,j}$ is the original score value for country i and variable j individual variable.
$\mathrm{INS}_{i,j}$ is the original score value for country i and variable j institutional variable.
$z_{i,j}$ is the calculated pillar value for country i and pillar j.

3. *Normalization:* Pillar values were first normalized to a range from 0 to 1, according to Eq. 6.2:

$$x_{i,j} = \frac{z_{i,j}}{\max z_{i,j}} \tag{6.2}$$

for all $j = 1, \ldots, k$, the number of pillars.
where:
$x_{i,j}$ is the normalized score value for country i and pillar j.
$\max z_{i,j}$ is the maximum value for pillar j.

4. *Capping:* All index building is based on a benchmarking principle. We selected the 95th percentile score adjustment, meaning that any observed values higher than the 95th percentile are lowered to the 95th percentile. For the 132 countries

[7] In order to check potential bias, the index was calculated without these countries; however, the GEI values and the rank order of the involved countries were basically unchanged.

in our dataset, we use the benchmark values from the full dataset, which contains all the 629 observations made over the 2002–2014 time period.

5. *Average pillar adjustment:* The different averages of the normalized values of the indicators imply that reaching the same indicator values requires different efforts and resources. Since we want to apply the GEI for public policy purposes, the additional resources for the same marginal improvement of the indicator values should be the same for all indicators. Therefore, we need a transformation to equate the average values of the components. Equation 6.3 shows the calculation of the average value of pillar *j*:

$$\overline{x}_j = \frac{\sum_{i=1}^{n} x_{i,j}}{n} \quad \text{for all } j \tag{6.3}$$

We want to transform the $x_{i,j}$ values such that the potential minimum value is 0 and the maximum value is 1:

$$y_{i,j} = x_{i,j}^{k} \tag{6.4}$$

where k is the "strength of adjustment" and the kth moment of x_j is exactly the needed average, $\overline{y}_j$.

We have to find the root of the following equation for k:

$$\sum_{i=1}^{n} x_{i,j}^{k} - n\overline{y}_j = 0 \tag{6.5}$$

It is easy to see, based on previous conditions and derivatives, that the function is decreasing and convex, which means it can be solved quickly using the well-known Newton-Raphson method with an initial guess of 0. After obtaining k, the computations are straightforward. Note that if

$$\overline{x}_j < \overline{y}_j \quad k < 1$$

$$\overline{x}_j = \overline{y}_j \quad k = 1$$

$$\overline{x}_j > \overline{y}_j \quad k > 1$$

then k is thought of as the strength (and direction) of adjustment.

The adjusted pillar values are calculated for all the 2002–2014 time period; these values and this distribution are applied for the 132 countries in the GEI 2016 edition. It means that the average adjusted pillar values of the countries that participated in the 2014 GEM cycle are exactly same in the 2002–2014 dataset and in the GEI 2016 edition. Note that, of the individual variables of the 132 countries in the GEI 2016 edition, 69 are from the 2013 survey, 29 are from earlier GEM surveys, and 34 are estimates.

6. *Penalizing:* After these transformations, the PFB methodology was used to create indicator-adjusted PFB values. We define our penalty function as follows:

$$h_{(i),j} = \min y_{(i),j} + \left(1 - e^{-\left(y_{(i)j} - \min y_{(i),j}\right)}\right) \tag{6.6}$$

where:

$h_{i,j}$ is the modified, post-penalty value of pillar j in country i.
$y_{i,j}$ is the normalized value of index component j in country i.
$y_{\min}$ is the lowest value of $y_{i,j}$ for country i.
$i = 1, 2, \ldots, n$ is the number of countries.
$j = 1, 2, \ldots, m$ is the number of pillars.

7. The pillars are the basic building blocks of the sub-index: entrepreneurial attitudes, entrepreneurial abilities, and entrepreneurial aspirations. The value of a sub-index for any country is the arithmetic average of its PFB-adjusted pillars for that sub-index, multiplied by 100. The maximum value of the sub-indices is 100, and the potential minimum is 0, both of which reflect the relative position of a country in a particular sub-index.

$$\text{ATT}_i = 100\sum_{j=1}^{5} \frac{h_j}{5} \tag{6.7a}$$

$$\text{ABT}_i = 100\sum_{j=6}^{9} \frac{h_j}{4} \tag{6.7b}$$

$$\text{ASP}_i = 100\sum_{j=10}^{14} \frac{h_j}{5} \tag{6.7c}$$

where:

$h_{i,j}$ is the modified, post-penalty value of pillar j in country i.
$i = 1, 2, \ldots, n$ is the number of countries.
$j = 1, 2, \ldots, 14$ is the number of pillars.

8. The super-index, the Global Entrepreneurship and Development Index, is simply the average of the three sub-indices. Since 100 represents the theoretically available limit, the GEI points can also be interpreted as a measure of the efficiency of the entrepreneurship resources:

$$\text{GEI}_i = \frac{1}{3}\left(\text{ATT}_i + \text{ABT}_i + \text{ASP}_i\right) \tag{6.8}$$

where $i = 1, 2, \ldots, n$ is the number of countries.

Recently, we report not only the GEI scores but also the associated measurement error terms for those countries that have participated in the GEM survey (see Chap. 2). It is impossible to make an error calculation for the countries that have only estimated individual data. The report of the confidence intervals is important in two respects. First, when comparing different countries, we can see if the differences in the two countries' GEI scores are significant or not. Based on the 2018 GEI scores, the GEI scores of the first nine countries—the United States, Switzerland, Canada, United Kingdom, Australia, Denmark, Iceland, Ireland, and Sweden,—do not differ significantly. However, the GEI score difference is significant between the United States in first place and France in tenth. Second, from year to year, we can see if changes in the GEI scores are significant or if they perhaps are due to measurement error.

The confidence interval calculation is based on the error terms of the Total Early-Phased Entrepreneurship Activity index, as reported by the GEM each year. An important note is that the real measurement error is unknown, since we use many data from different sources for which confidence intervals are not currently available. Keep in mind that the real measurement errors are higher than the values reported here.

The Underlying Structure of the Data: Reflecting the Full 2006–2016 Dataset

While the number of composite indicators has been increasing over the last few decades, some index creators pay little attention to the interrelationship between the different variables. Although the PFB methodology provides a practical solution for how to take this interrelationship into account, it does not save us from examining the underlying structure of the data. It is particularly important to have a well-defined nested structure of the whole index. The arbitrary selection of the variables—in our case the pillars—would cause confusion, false interpretation, and, finally, a misleading policy interpretation. The OECD handbook of composite indicators recommends analyzing the dataset in two dimensions, pillars and countries.[8] We have already provided detailed analyses at the country level; here we are presenting a pillar-level analysis by calculating the common (Pearson) correlation coefficients. Since we have only estimated data from 35 countries, it is better to examine not the 137 countries involved in our analysis but the full 2006–2016 dataset, with 619 data points excluding the estimated country data.

We report correlations between the normalized and average equalized pillars, shown in Table 6.6, and the correlations between the normalized indicators after applying the PFB methodology, shown in Table 6.7. In general, significant and

[8] OECD (2008).

Table 6.6 The correlation matrix between the normalized and average equated pillars (2006–2016 dataset)

		1	2	3	4	5	6	7	8	9	10	11	12	13	14
1	Opportunity perception	1	.513**	.620**	.578**	.831**	.741**	.516**	.456**	.672**	.450**	.412**	.467**	.387**	.464**
2	Startup skills		1	.473**	.424**	.554**	.551**	.520**	.390**	.424**	.312**	.414**	.308**	.423**	.473**
3	Risk acceptance			1	.520**	.702**	.773**	.641**	.579**	.681**	.528**	.688**	.518**	.557**	.620**
4	Networking				1	.612**	.604**	.419**	.361**	.490**	.514**	.480**	.401**	.283**	.476**
5	Cultural support					1	.821**	.627**	.519**	.733**	.535**	.572**	.572**	.514**	.643**
6	Opportunity startup						1	.701**	.651**	.764**	.558**	.699**	.559**	.623**	.709**
7	Technology absorption							1	.534**	.609**	.527**	.712**	.578**	.616**	.654**
8	Human capital								1	.554**	.471**	.542**	.638**	.517**	.602**
9	Competition									1	.505**	.616**	.481**	.552**	.577**
10	Product innovation										1	.634**	.637**	.465**	.605**
11	Process innovation											1	.574**	.655**	.686**
12	High growth												1	.573**	.635**
13	Internationalization													1	.655**
14	Risk capital														1
	** Correlation is significant at the 0.01 level (two-tailed)														
	The number of observations= 619														

Table 6.7 The correlation matrix between the indicators, sub-Indices, and the GEI super-index after normalizing and applying the PFB method (2006–2016 dataset)

		2	3	4	5	6	7	8	9	10	11	12	13	14	15	16	17	18
1	Opportunity perception	.628**	.715**	.676**	.869**	.896**	.801**	.635**	.597**	.761**	.785**	.588**	.560**	.605**	.538**	.591**	.658**	.815**
2	Startup skills	1	.609**	.565**	.671**	.804**	.679**	.655**	.557**	.579**	.696**	.491**	.575**	.502**	.575**	.621**	.635**	.745**
3	Risk acceptance		1	.648**	.780**	.879**	.830**	.725**	.674**	.765**	.842**	.652**	.763**	.634**	.662**	.709**	.784**	.875**
4	Networking			1	.707**	.816**	.704**	.568**	.510**	.616**	.675**	.628**	.610**	.540**	.445**	.603**	.646**	.745**
5	Cultural support				1	.931**	.864**	.727**	.642**	.810**	.856**	.662**	.692**	.685**	.644**	.733**	.781**	.896**
6	ATTINDEX					1	.899**	.770**	.694**	.819**	.895**	.698**	.745**	.688**	.669**	.756**	.814**	.945**
7	Opportunity startup						1	.770**	.736**	.823**	.936**	.673**	.781**	.663**	.713**	.776**	.827**	.930**
8	Technology absorption							1	.647**	.702**	.883**	.638**	.783**	.690**	.705**	.746**	.816**	.863**
9	Human capital								1	.664**	.848**	.600**	.643**	.718**	.636**	.707**	.754**	.803**
10	Competition									1	.893**	.629**	.718**	.610**	.657**	.680**	.755**	.862**
11	ABTINDEX										1	.714**	.824**	.752**	.763**	.818**	.887**	.972**
12	Product innovation											1	.719**	.711**	.599**	.703**	.850**	.791**
13	Process innovation												1	.672**	.736**	.771**	.896**	.862**
14	High growth													1	.675**	.724**	.858**	.804**
15	Internationalization														1	.740**	.862**	.803**
16	Risk capital															1	.904**	.867**
17	ASPINDEX																1	.945**
18	GEI																	1
	** Correlation is significant at the 0.01 level (two-tailed)																	
	The number of observations = 619																	

medium to high correlations exist between the pillars in both cases. The lowest correlation is between networking and internationalization (0.283), and the highest is between opportunity perception and cultural support (0.831).

The PFB pillars, as can be expected, improved the correlation, implying a closer relationship between the entrepreneurial features. The positive connection between the entrepreneurship pillars is vital for proper policy interpretation and suggestions. If the connection between the pillars were negative, it would have implied that one pillar can only be improved at the cost of the other pillar. In this case, the improvement of the weakest pillar value would not be necessary to improve the GEI value. This is not the case.

There are other ways to check out the consistency of the dataset and the potentially strong connection between the pillars. Both the Kaiser-Meyer-Olkin measure of sampling adequacy and Bartlett's test of sphericity reinforce the fact that the 14 GEI pillars are closely correlated, and it is worth looking for a single complex measure.[9] The most popular test of the internal consistency of the pillars is based on the Cronbach coefficient alpha (c-alpha). The c-alpha value for the 14 pillars is 0.95 with the original data and 0.97 after applying the PFB methodology; both are well above the critical 0.7 threshold value.[10] In sum, all of these tests support the internal consistency of the structure as described with the 14 selected pillars.

Summary

In this chapter, we have described the index-building methodology and the dataset. The GEI, a complex index reflecting the multidimensional nature of entrepreneurship, consists of 3 sub-indices, 14 pillars, and 31 variables. While some researchers insist on simple entrepreneurship indicators, none of the previously applied measures was able to explain the role of entrepreneurship in economic development with a single indicator.

Our index-building logic differs from other widely applied indices in three respects: it incorporates both individual and institutional variables, it equalizes the 14 pillar values for equalizing the marginal effects, and it takes into account the weakest link in the system. The institutional variables can also be viewed as country-specific weighting factors. Moreover, institutional variables can balance out the potential inconsistency of the GEM data collection. The weakest link refers to the

---

[9] The Kaiser-Meyer-Olkin measures for the original pillar values are 0.94 and 0.96 for the PFB-adjusted pillars, well above the critical value of 0.50. The Bartlett's test is significant at the 0.000 level, excluding the possibility that the pillars are not interrelated.

[10] We have calculated the c-alpha values for each of the three sub-indices. Using the PFB-adjusted pillar values, the c-alpha scores are 0.92 (ATT pillars), 0.91 (ABT pillars), and 0.93 (ASP pillars).

decreased performance effect of the bottleneck. Practically speaking, it means that the higher pillar values are adjusted to the weakest performing pillar value. While the exact measure of the penalty is unknown, meaning that the solution is not necessarily optimal, it still provides a better solution than calculating the simple arithmetic averages. Consequently, the newly developed PFB can be applied in cases where an imperfect substitutability exists among the variables and the efficiency of the system depends on the weakest performing variable. The method is particularly useful in making policy suggestions.

The GEM survey served as a source for the individual variables, which are calculated mainly from the 2015–2016 individual dataset, except for the 35 countries that only have data from previous years. Altogether, the sample includes 529,466 individuals from 102 countries. Individual data from 35 other countries are estimated by using similar or nearby country individual data, resulting in a sample size of 137 countries. Precaution is advised in any cases where estimated or pre-2013 GEM survey individual data are applied.

The availability of the institutional variables for all the countries has limited our selection possibilities. The proper interpretation of a particular institutional variable has been an important aspect of the selection. In this new version of GEI, we increased the number of institutional indicators that have resulted in an improvement of the internal consistency of the dataset as well as provided a wider aspect of describing the national system of entrepreneurship. In all cases, we used the most recent institutional data available as of May, 31, 2017.

We summarized the index-building steps in eight points. Since these steps were described in full detail in the previous publications, we provided only a short description.[11]

We have analyzed the underlying structure of the dataset in the variable level. The correlation coefficients, the Kaiser-Meyer-Olkin measures, and the Bartlett's and c-alpha tests all suggested that the 14 pillars have a close relation to one another and that there is a place to construct a composite indicator. These tests were executed with the normalized original as well as with the PFB-adjusted variables. As expected, the PFB methodology improved the internal consistency of the dataset.

References

Acs, Z. J., & Szerb, L. (2009). The Global Entrepreneurship Index (GEINDEX). *Foundations and Trends in Entrepreneurship, 5*, 341–435.

Acs, Z. J., & Szerb, L. (2012). *Global Entrepreneurship Index* (p. 400). Cheltenham, UK: Edward Elgar.

[11]Acs, Rappai, and Szerb (2011), Acs, Autio, and Szerb (2014).

Acs, Z. J., Rappai, G. & Szerb, L. (2011, October 17). Index-building in a system of interdependent variables: The penalty for bottleneck. GMU School of Public Policy Research Paper No. 2011-24. Available at SSRN: http://ssrn.com/abstract=1945346.

Acs, Z. J., Szerb, L., & Autio, E. (2013). *Global Entrepreneurship Index* (p. 352). Cheltenham, UK: Edward Elgar.

Acs, Z. J., Szerb, L., & Autio, E. (2014). *The Global Entrepreneurship Index 2014.* Seattle: CreateSpace.

Acs, Z. J., Autio, E., & Szerb, L. (2014). *National Systems of Entrepreneurship: Policy and Measurement issues, Research Policy, 43*(3), 476–494.

Acs, Z. J., Szerb, L., & Autio, E. (2016). *The Global Entrepreneurship Index 2015.* Cham: Springer International Publishing.

Autio, E., & Levie, J. (2015). *Management of entrepreneurial ecosystems.* Mimeo: Imperial college Business School.

Estoniareport.(2015).TowardsamoreentrepreneurialEstonia:Callforaction,GlobalEntrepreneurship and Development Institute, https://thegedi.org/estonia-regional-facilitation-report/.

Groh, A., Liechtenstein, H., & Lieser, K. (2012a). *The global venture capital and private equity country attractiveness index, 2012.*

Groh, A., Liechtenstein, H., & Lieser, K. (2012b). *The global venture capital and private equity country attractiveness index.*http://blog.iese.edu/vcpeindex/about/.

OECD/European Commission/Joint Research Centre (OECD). (2008). *Handbook on constructing composite indicators: Methodology and user guide.* Paris: OECD.

MIX
Papier aus verantwortungsvollen Quellen
Paper from responsible sources
FSC® C105338

If you have any concerns about our products,
you can contact us on
ProductSafety@springernature.com

In case Publisher is established outside the EU,
the EU authorized representative is:
Springer Nature Customer Service Center GmbH
Europaplatz 3, 69115 Heidelberg, Germany

Printed by Libri Plureos GmbH
in Hamburg, Germany